Your Guest is as good as mine

Mike Fry

Table of Contents

Acknowledgements – page 6
Dedication – page 7
Forward – page 8

Chapter 1 – page 9
'Guests - *running a B&B without them would be so much easier'*

Chapter 2 – page 13
'I could write a book about these bloody people'

Chapter 3 – page 16
'a chink in the armour'

Chapter 4 – page 20
'there is but one constant'

Chapter 5 – page 23
'there's good news and bad news'

Chapter 6 – page 28
'there are nutters everywhere'

Chapter 7 – page 31
'open your wallet and say after me, help yourself'

Chapter 8 – page 36
'a sale is not a sale until the money is in the bank'

Chapter 9 – page 40
'do not under-estimate the cost of restoring old houses'

Chapter 10 – page 45
'Shit! – what have we done'

Chapter 11 – page 51
'do ghosts eat chocolate?'

Chapter 12 – page 57
'F O Henry's gold would come in handy'

Chapter 13 – page 66
'another trip to the bank'

Chapter 14 – page 72
'Rob had a look of horror on his face'

Chapter 15 – page 77
'cold showers and no mirror'

Chapter 16 – page 81
'to boldly go where no other guesthouse has gone'

Chapter 17 – page 85
'where's your fucking note?'

Chapter 18 – page 89
'they were disguised as guests'

Chapter 19 – page 96
'a right royal rogering'

Chapter 20 – page 99
'they've been out there breeding'

Chapter 21 – page 103
'wash those dishes, scrub those pots'

Chapter 22 – page 108
'Darwin's theory of evolution'

Chapter 23 – page 111
'we may meet again one day'

Chapter 24 – page 114
'a few words of advice'

Chapter 25 – page 123
'you're the bloody spoon salesman'

Chapter 26 – page 126
'more advice'

Chapter 27 – page 129
'a collection of stories'

Chapter 28 – page 143
'things that go bump in the night'

Chapter 29 – page 151
'a breath of fresh air'

Chapter 30 – page 156
'I booked a room with water views'

Chapter 31 – page 164
'one nip or three and other indiscretions'

Chapter 32 – page 174
'Chefs, noisy kitchens and trainees'

Chapter 33 – page 181
'you just had to be there'

Chapter 34 – page 207
'rats, banks and paid companions'

Chapter 35 – page 216
'a couple of memorable B&Bs'

Chapter 36 – page 218
'are you really cut out for this job'

Chapter 37 – page 226
'be a team player and join in'

Chapter 38 – page 233
'reviews – a love hate relationship'

Chapter 39 – page 237
'OTAs – online travel agents'

Chapter 40 – page 241
'make the internet work for you'

About the Author – page 247

ISBN 978-0-9758482-3-4

Acknowledgements:

I wish to thank my long-suffering partner Carolyn without whom the business would not have been as successful as it was. Whilst we were both tolerating the guests, she was also tolerating me. During the course of our tenure at Ormiston House we made many new friends while at the same time retaining our old friends despite rarely having the time to spend with them that we would have liked.

Special thanks go to those friends and business colleagues who is some shape or form have enabled me to write this book and who have contributed in some way. The list is extensive however in particular I would like to specifically mention the following people. In saying that none of these people should be blamed for any of the profanity or unsavoury commentary; in that respect I must take full responsibility.

Cover by Ange @ pro_ebookcovers

Crichton McIntyre, William Upfield, Desma Pacitto, Marilyn Risdale, Lorraine Gardener, Wally Lynd, Peta Fry, Stephanie Nissen, Danielle O'Meara, Alan O'Meara, Tara Mitchell, Tanya Gmelic, Andrew Dishington, The Grining Family, Jodi and Michael Stacey, Christine and Quenton Higgs, Jan Buckingham, Joy Chappell, Anthony Coulson, Richard and Nigel Morgan, Brenda Egan, The restoration crew of Rob Brown, Col Heron, Kurt Hartnell, Colin and Joyce Gayle and family, Mark, Andrew, Clem Ludby, Bobby Jones, Steve McGuiness, Tut Ludby, Flash Ludby, Kevin Bailey, Photographer Bruce Hutchison and others. Our dear deceased dog Tiffany who kept us sane while she was with us. I know there are many more and to those I apologise if I have missed you.

for

Rob Hassall

Loyal friend, fellow skipper, business partner
and a true gentleman. We miss you Rob.

Forward

Anyone who has owned or operated a hospitality business could easily write an account of their experiences. In that, I am not unique. In fact, just dealing with the general public brings forth a host of probabilities, incidents and near misses for any aspiring author to recount. This is an assembly of just some of my experiences and of a few of my industry colleagues. Not all tourism and hospitality people are willing to vent their experiences publicly; save for moments among their colleagues when they relate, perhaps, the affairs of the day. I make no apologies for some of the language used and in fact have cleaned a lot of it up over the many rewrites and edits. Not for the sake of some clinical vivisection of profanity but purely in an effort to tell the tales without the appearance of a rant. Language in the community has changed dramatically over the years and some words, previously taboo in normal conversation are now commonplace. Profanity behind the scenes in hospitality businesses has been the long suit for many years. Let's face it even Custer would have said "Jesus Christ, look at all those fuckin' Indians."

I am reminded of a quote by Ernest Hemmingway.

"I've tried to reduce profanity, but I reduced so much profanity when writing the book that I'm afraid not much could come out. Perhaps we will have to consider it simply as a profane book and hope that the next book will be less profane or perhaps more sacred. "

If anyone reading this book has ever worked in hospitality, tourism or any aspect of dealing with the general public then I am sure you, at least, will see where the narrative is coming from. Generally speaking, this book is not about you. It is about those other people; but how were we to know, they were disguised as guests

Chapter One

'Guests - running a B&B without them would be so much easier'

This little 'Facebook' gem was posted from a fellow tourism operator just before going to print. It is now very apparent that the terminally stupid are in fact breeding.

Ok come on; being a tourist doesn't mean you have to be a complete moron. As most of you know we now own and operate the (removed) and we live on the premises. This comes with its own set of experiences and challenges. Yesterday I decided to do an hour or two of some lo-o-o-ng awaited gardening. As I was going to be right down the back, I left a sign on the office door, thinking this will do the trick: "The office is currently unattended. If you require assistance I am in the garden. Or call this number, etc." So, a guest saw the sign, still came into the office, ignored the sign on the desk that said if you require assistance please press doorbell. Then ignored the sign on the next door, which is the door to our private residence that says, "staff only". Helped themselves through that door and wandered around our home. Opened another door to find my daughter and her young baby in the lounge room doing their private stuff. Without saying anything they then closed the door and took themselves out. Luckily Bobby (dog) didn't go for them. I think he was as dumb founded as Bianca was. I'm not sure what they wanted but they didn't call the number or come back so couldn't have been too urgent. Please give me strength 😬 😬

I recall an incident somewhat similar a few years ago.

One day, not so long ago, I was conducting a severe pruning of an old Camellia which had grown into a tree but with quite a bit of die back. The leaves in the old extremities were yellow and it was a job that was begging to be done. I doctored another old one beside it a few years previously and it came good, almost by divine intervention. So, after a full day's work and a few trips to the refuse station I stripped off and threw the dirty work clothes in the wash basket and popped into the shower. As I was getting into the shower I looked out of the window and there was a couple, possibly late sixties, walking around our private area. For fuck's sake, I thought, we have 1.4 acres of gardens and most of it is devoted to bloody house guests, and fucking nosy parkers, and now we have these two individuals poking around our private space. Realistically they could have seen my naked body and were perhaps beating a hasty retreat. I mumble a few words of profanity and get the dirt, bark and general garden rubbish off my body.

As I get out of the shower cubicle Carolyn calls me from out in our garden and I yell out that I am naked and wet from the shower. The calling continues so I walk out of the bathroom and nearly stand on the biggest blue tongue lizard

I have ever seen sunning himself on the carpet in front of one of the windows, inside the house. So, dripping wet and totally naked, I pick him up [blue tongues are great for the garden and despite their ferocious demeanour are quite ok to pick up] and meet Caro at the back door of our apartment. "You'll never believe what just happened," says Carolyn with an air of incredulity, and not the least bit surprised that I am dripping wet, standing totally naked and holding an extremely large blue tongue lizard at the same time.

Caro tells me that this couple walked in through our private entrance calling out and eventually, after walking around the entire perimeter of the house, finally arrived at the front door. As their journey started in the tradesman's entrance, clearly marked as such, and had walked around from the back, they did not trip the main sensor in the driveway, so we had no idea they were wandering around.

"We see you have a vacancy." Comment by gormless member of the public.

"No, I'm sorry, [we're not really sorry, but we say that] we are full [which we were]." Reply from weary female guesthouse owner

"But your vacancy sign says that you have a vacancy." Further comment by traveller together with surprisingly vacant look.

So, Caro again apologises and says no we don't and walks to the front gate in company with the recalcitrant tourists and sure enough the 'No Vacancy' sign is out and hanging on the fence adjacent to the driveway, and the Vacancy board has been brought inside and hidden behind a tree. It was my job to bring the vacancy sign in that day when we sold our last room a few hours earlier.

Caro initially thought that I must have left the sign out on the footpath. If I had then this rapidly developing incident would have had apocalyptic consequences for myself. However, the ever-observant Carolyn notices that the tourists had parked their car at the side of the house and had not in fact driven into our main driveway. The tourists say "There's the sign...it says 'Vacancy' with an arrow pointing to our back entrance"

Now this removable sign is inside the fence and behind a tree and is totally invisible when driving past. They would have had to stop the car and walk into the garden to see this sign.

Now most normal people would know that when a property has a vacancy, they put a sign outside the entrance or on the footpath saying Vacancy. When the property is full, they bring it in and put it inside the property out of sight of visitors and replace it with a 'No Vacancy' sign.

Apparently, we have got it wrong. If there is a sign anywhere on your property, even hidden behind a tree, in a shed or locked in the garage and it says Vacancy then you must have a vacancy. If the visitor can find the sign, then that means there is a vacant room. It is like a combination of a Monopoly board game and Where's Wally. So following this event I was tasked with finding a hiding place for this fucking sign so that the terminally stupid don't think we have a vacancy even though we have a 'No Vacancy' sign hanging on the main entrance; but if they rummage around the garden they might be able to find a sign that says we do have a vacancy. I ask you …….

There is an exceedingly good chance that the language in this book may deteriorate so there will be a little more profanity to follow, if that does not offend, please read on.

Regardless, the warning has been given. Let's call that a disclaimer.

I must point out at this early stage that ninety-nine point nine per cent of guests are fine. Some are a little odd and some are a tad impolite. In some cases, this could also apply to hosts or staff; relax, I am sure this book is not about you.

Chapter Two

'I could write a book about these bloody people'

In 1999, four years after purchasing our forlorn and neglected mansion, I self-published a small book on Ormiston House. It was an account of the restoration of the house, the history of the Henry family who built it and how we had positioned ourselves as a premier guesthouse within the Tasmanian west coast tourism scene. I used a

Tasmanian publishing firm to arrange proofing and printing and within a short space of time we had five thousand copies at Ormiston House ready and for sale. I sent a box to the local visitor's centre and another to one of the cruise companies for them to sell. The in-house sales were steady and most of our sales were directly to house guests who took away the book as a souvenir. The original idea of writing a book came from two sources. One was from a trip I did to the UK in 1998 where I noticed that most, if not all, of the stately homes and historical locations had a small booklet explaining the history and other important aspects of the house or locality. The other was from the house guests themselves who would continually, and understandably, enquire about the house, us, the family who built it and also ask if we had any written material we could give them; so the idea was borne to write exactly what the customer required, as requested and as evidenced during my travels to the UK.

In fact, it was also because I was getting very tired of telling the same story, many times each day, day after day, year after year. I have no doubt they found my storytelling fascinating, but I needed to get some relief from the constant repetition.

The project, I must say, was greeted most enthusiastically by the guests and our fellow tourism operators. Whenever we had an in-house tour of travel consultants, we would give each of them a copy to read and to use as a reference. Remember this all happened in 1999, some years before the internet took centre stage and four years after we embarked on this venture. A lot happened in that time which you will find out very shortly.

We sent personally signed and addressed copies of the book to the mainland Tasmanian Travel Centres. We also sent a copy to the area sales managers from Tourism Tasmania as well as those within the state tourism organisation that were directly involved in selling tourism product to the mainland and the world. This included the 'state run' tourism wholesaler Tasmania's Temptations Holidays. These were the days before online bookings; the days when only a small percentage of tourism operators had an email address. Very few had a website and online travel agents were a thing of the future and Google was a fledgling search engine. The Ormiston House Book became a substantial contributor to our success. Almost immediately guests would comment on the quality of the booklet and the story. They also complimented me on the writing which I found flattering of course. We published a second edition in 2006 and another five thousand copies.

Around this same time, 1999, sitting on my laptop, was the start of a book I thought would be a good idea. I called it 'Your Guest is as Good as Mine'. From the time we opened the business I thought to myself "I could write a book about these bloody people," referring to difficult and odd guests as well as the behind the scenes tragedies that seemed to play out almost daily. I probably first started it in the form of a digital diary in about 1997 after a series of unfortunate events that I needed to vent. It then progressed to writing observations of human nature. It soon became obvious that writing about negative experiences was perhaps not the way to go. My pages were full of expletives and I found myself ranting about the day's activities. In some ways reading them back was therapeutical and made me smile but the language was atrocious. The thought of producing an 'R' rated publication crossed my mind. At one point I decided that it would be better to only write after I had a 'really good' day; I went weeks without writing anything.... Another strategy was required.

Chapter Three

'a chink in the armour'

I often wonder how many people consider how wonderful or exciting it would be to run a bed and breakfast business. A great deal more, I feel, than take that tangible leap and thus embark upon a paradigm shift into the great unknown.
I am not just talking about opening a room in your house to the occasional guest or turning the granny flat out the back into an Airbnb. I am talking about a significant change of

lifestyle together with what could be an even more significant investment in a new and virtually unknown industry to many people. It is one thing to stay in a quaint little B & B and quite another to own and operate one; in that respect, for some of my erstwhile peers, the smaller the better. In another respect, and if profit is a motive, then something more substantial will be required; but are you up to the task I ask?

Take us for example. For twenty-one years, 1995-2016, co-running a notable Tasmanian guesthouse and bed and breakfast with partner Carolyn, and now writing a tome that has been a work in progress for about the last eighteen years. One reason for the structural longevity of this composition could be the constant interruptions from guests and another could be the frustrations dealing with some of those same esteemed patrons. Another reason, and this is purely personal, is finding the most acceptable language and attitude to produce this work and to accommodate that which has played such a considerable role in my life.

I am sure, in fact I know, that I am not the only hospitality person that has a story to tell. I, like many of my industry peers, have a range of stories from the downright hilarious to the absolute horrific. This book is but a peek behind the scenes; a chink in the armour of that brave facade we wear in the face of battling with the general public.

Our story started with a holiday to Tasmania. We fell in love with a derelict federation mansion that we decided to restore and renovate; in reflection a little too much passion and too little capital. This can be a danger when emotion and passion play a bigger role than pragmatic common sense. Notwithstanding we proceeded and here we are twenty-five years after the purchase, and we are still a couple; so, it doesn't always end in total disaster. However, we did have our stumbles, laughs, tears and oh yes....'guests' along the way. There were financial institutions to deal with but despite those bastards we stayed in business, but it was not a walk in the park.

An easier option than total restoration would have been to buy an existing business and have the benefit of instant cash flow instead of instant expenditure. Instant cash flow also helps to tolerate instant guests. Most of them will be wonderful; some of them won't be. You will wonder why some of them even bothered to come on holidays. Most will have a smile on their faces and engage with a friendly and courteous manner; others will whinge and complain about everything from the weather to the terrible roads as soon as they set foot in your commodious establishment. Some will shake your hand as if they are greeting old friends they have not seen for years while others will shrug past you as if you were a piece of furniture. Some will hug you and thank you for a wonderful time when they leave and there will be others who sneak out without saying goodbye or merely grunt when you wish them well for their journey. After some leave, you will close the door and say, "thank goodness they have gone." If you are like me you would say, "thank fuck they're gone; now some other poor bastard can have them."

For us there were some issues during the restoration and realistically not unexpected. It was a combination; a 'sweet and sour' time for us, but on reflection, overall, we enjoyed restoring the house. Would we do it again? Emphatically no. We had a five to ten-year plan and then we were heading back to Brisbane. It didn't quite work out that way and in the end, we loved Tasmania so much we decided to stay after we sold. That is not to say we didn't enjoy running the business, we did. I think it is something that if embarked upon, in the manner in which we did, then you will only do it once in a lifetime regardless of the duration.

As for the guests? We forged some wonderful friendships over the years and made so many promises to visit many of them one day. Unfortunately, when operating a B&B, 24/7, 365 days of the year, it is difficult to get away let alone go on an extended holiday. There were also those that we would prefer to forget, but I can't so it's time to tell you about some of them.

Getting this book finished was not an easy task. Try as I may I seemed to have one priority after another take precedence during the days and weeks. Bear in mind that when running a 5-bedroom B & B, the owners do not just sit around waiting for someone to ring the doorbell as some of our guests seem to think we do. We have a sensor on the driveway so that we can get to the front door before they do but believe me, we do not sit at a desk in the foyer reading magazines, waiting for them to arrive. Running a B & B will give you the unique privilege of working 24/7 and that will be continuous unless you have vacancies or deliberately choose to locate your B & B in a destination that is seasonal enough for you to easily take a break. In our case Strahan has patronage all year round although the winters [June, July, and August] can be quiet enough that you may not lose too much business if you close for a few weeks. So, if you are up and running at say 6am and the "buggars" go to bed by 10pm that is 16 hours, multiplied by 7 is 112 hrs. Mind you it would be sensible to pace yourself and get some "me' time during the day. This is a lifestyle business so make sure both you and your guests don't stuff it up for you.

Chapter Four

'there is but one constant'

Getting away from a busy B&B can be difficult. There are options of course but when advance bookings can be up to twelve months ahead, finding a hole big enough to accommodate a holiday can be difficult. Closing off for a period is an option however if like us you contract with wholesale suppliers then taking your property out of the system when you are listed as available in brochures, websites etc. is not greeted well. Closing off also creates issues with cash flow especially when the bills keep rolling in. For many years Carolyn and I would slip away separately while the other held the fort; not ideal but necessary at times.

Employing managers and locums has its risks and expenses. Finding the right people to take care of your property, reputation and guests is also a risky business. If you already employ staff some of them may be able to rise to the occasion but usually only for short periods of time. It must be remembered that hosted accommodation requires a host on site effectively 24/7.

The customer is always right? Really? Emphatically 'no'. We have Harry Gordon Selfridge to thank for that statement. Quite frankly the public can be a pain in the backside at times, in fact frequently. At times they can also be dishonest. You would think that when people go on holiday, they would be different, more 'easy going', friendly, light-hearted and honest.

Bed and Breakfast operations are a little different than other forms of accommodation. They are usually hosted and have a high level of interaction. That in effect creates an environment prone to incidents. Over the years I have known many B & B operators and I have found them to be wonderful people; some are odd and eccentric, and some may have thought that about us as well. Most of them think, as we did, that they do a great job and run a very professional business; most of them do, some don't.

For those reading this book who are considering purchasing or setting up a 'bed and breakfast' style operation I wish you good fortune and trust you maintain your sense of humour. Whilst we had a sound background in tourism and hospitality, we also made some errors of judgement that cost us dearly. At the end of the day if it feels good you will do it, and most will do well. There are, however, some warning signs that you would do well to heed.

For those of you reading this book, and have stayed at a B & B, who would like to know what your host thinks of you, congratulations your wish may be granted; especially if you exhibited some nasty habits. For those owners of B & Bs who are reading this book and disagree with anything or gasping in abject horror at my frank and brutal honesty don't call me, go and write your own bloody book; if you can find the time between servicing rooms and pandering to the whims of your esteemed clientele.

The world is changing; hospitality and tourism are no exceptions. The internet has revolutionised the way in which we research and book our holidays and recently the sharing economy has brought even more changes and created as many challenges as benefits. There is but one constant – the guest.

Chapter Five

'there's good news and bad news'

Our venture into the bed and breakfast world was both accidental and brutally quick. In hindsight it would have been more prudent to think the whole scenario over for longer than we did but a strange sequence of events occurred starting with a holiday to Tasmania and a love affair with a forlorn and neglected Federation mansion.

As it turned out both my work history, and that of my partner Carolyn, played an integral role in our decision to venture into a B & B. Please forgive this slight digression, it helps to see where our temporary insanity came from.

You can skip the "history and house restoration section" if you want to go directly through to guest related experiences and incidents. Just go to Chapter 15, much more profanity once the guests arrived.

Initially, my background was navy where I was a radar operator and, when I left the navy in 1975, I was a petty officer air controller and instructor. Following departure from the navy, I ventured into my parent's retail supermarket in Rockhampton Queensland. That period lasted two and a half years before my relationship with my father reached a point where we had to go separate ways. I then worked for Uncle Bens as the central Queensland representative selling pet food to supermarkets and grocery stores. That employment lasted 2 years and I felt I was done with the supermarket thing, so I joined the airport fire and rescue service at the Rockhampton Airport.

After another eighteen months waiting for an aircraft to crash (thankfully, it never did while I was there), a position came up for a sales manager with Bush Pilot Airways for the start of their Great Keppel Island air service and as the base manager for the airline at Rocky airport. I got the job almost immediately having had sales and marketing experience and that I had already been working at, and familiar with, the airport for the previous eighteen months. After another eighteen months I was promoted and sent to Brisbane as the sales manager for south east Queensland. By this time my first marriage was over, and I moved south as a single man. Spending too much time on Great Keppel Island had something to do with that. By the middle of 1983 it was time for another change again.

The Brisbane Paddle Wheeler was a tremendously satisfying time in my life and gave me so much insight into operating a small tourism business. Rob and I were both skippers and did everything on the boat from greeting passengers to cleaning the bilges. We had a great crew and became the best of friends which continued even after my sudden departure and relocation to Tasmania. By 1995 we had put the Paddlewheeler on the market. Rob was sixty-two and felt it was time to have a break and I was forty-six and looking at life's next adventure.

Following twelve years on the Paddlewheeler, (1983-1995) and another failed marriage, I had a good grounding in the tourism industry and successfully dealing with the public. I can't say the same for marital relationships.

Although I did not know it at the time, one of the skills I acquired on the Paddlewheeler would hold me in good stead. That was, how to be rid of passengers who overstayed their welcome. In reflection the answer was quite simple, and Rob and I were absolutely gobsmacked when we realised the most effective technique. Just tell them to 'fuck off'.

We had a cruise with a university group and a small collection of self-professed intellectuals and future world leaders were hanging around the lower deck bar. Alison, one of our crew members came up to the bridge where Rob and I were getting the last payment out of the organiser, another Uni student. Alison complained that she could not get the last 'recalcitrants' off the boat. The organiser overheard her conversation so promptly said, "don't worry, come with me."

Alison returned a few minutes later and said, "All those years we have laboured over getting the last alcoholic stragglers off the boat and all we had to do is one thing."

"What's that?' we said.

"Just tell them to fuck off, (pause) and do you know what they did?"

"No, what?"

"They fucked off."

If only we had realised this sophisticated technique years earlier.

The trombonist in our jazz band, Tom Nicholson, also had an interesting way of clearing the boat at the end of the jazz cruise. "Thank you, ladies and gentlemen, there's good news and bad news. The good news is you don't have to go home, the bad news is you can't stay here, so piss off." The effect this had on the passengers was profound. They laughed and pissed off. Brilliant.

Just recently I was the reunion chief for our old navy radar group, and we had some guys who did not want to leave at the end of the function so I took a leaf out of Tom's book and gave them the good and bad news. Only this time I finished with "fuck off". To which they laughed, they then told me to fuck off, but they got the message and one by one they trickled out. The catering manager came over to me and said, "I've never heard that one before." She and her staff were pissing themselves.

Carolyn also had many years in hotel accommodation sales and marketing, with several companies, including Hilton International and some years before Thrifty Rent a car. I never heard her say "fuck" for many years. After a while dealing with the guests a few 'well chosen' words did creep out. By the time we sold the business; you guessed it, the vocabulary was up there with the best of them. The general public have an uncanny knack of generating behavioural metamorphisms.

Carolyn and I hooked up in early 1994. While we did not think we knew it all, we thought we had the right background to make a small accommodation and restaurant business work. In general terms we were correct. However, it did not prevent some serious issues surfacing during the first few years of operation. This is not unusual as anyone who has operated a business will tell you.

For us, it was a mixture of Tasmania, the house, the town of Strahan and the strange chemistry that seemed to weave those components together. From a strictly pecuniary perspective, and I think my financial advisor mentioned this, it would have been a better idea to stick with the cruise boat and Brisbane real estate than sell and invest in Tasmania. In 1995 our Brisbane money could buy us comparatively much more in Tasmanian real estate so in our minds at the time a '20 room' waterfront mansion for $425,000 was a bargain. Unfortunately, Brisbane's real estate market in early 1995 was not buoyant and very much a buyer's market. Selling our properties at the prices we wanted was going to be difficult.

Chapter Six

'there are nutters everywhere'

On our holiday in March 1995 we stayed at a variety of accommodation properties. My sister and brother-in-law had a travel agency in Newcastle, so we got them to do the itinerary and bookings. My brother-in-law, Quenton, is a Tasmanian so he knew more than we did about the state. That is one of the problems now with people booking online without touching base with the property...they end up missing out on so much by not getting some local knowledge about where to go and what to see along the way.

We flew over for a holiday and very nearly went straight back after I sat next to this loopy Tasmanian woman. Carolyn and Stephanie were on the other side of the aisle to the right and I was on the opposite aisle seat with this woman in the middle seat on my left.

She asked me if I was on holiday and I said yes. Then she said to me, "We all have two heads in Tasmania...I had an extra one, but I had it cut off...most of us do. I still have the scar...there's a little bump on my shoulder...you can feel it if you like."

There was no way I was going to feel the lady's lumps and bumps as I desperately looked for a vacant seat to escape to. There was also the consideration to immediately return to Queensland on the next available flight. After a frightening few seconds I figured her to be totally stupid and fortunately the majority of Tasmanians are great people with very little evidence of more than one head. There are 'nutters' everywhere, I concluded.

We started our holiday in Hobart and stayed with friends. This was great as they knew the place well and we got to see and do a heap of sightseeing. We then headed west with a two-night stopover in Strahan. We stayed at a little cottage called 'McIntosh Cottage' which was fantastic and some years later we in fact bought it and ran it for a while during a period of expansion and it was a nice little earner. After a few years of even more guests we sold the cottage. We must have had a lot of energy in those days, despite running the restaurant and accommodation as well.

Back to our holiday; even though it rained a fair bit this in no way detracted from the beauty of this area. In fact, we detected something special about Strahan. We remarked that it reminded us of Cabot Cove in 'Murder She Wrote'; we half expected Jessica Fletcher to toddle past on her bicycle.

The cruise was fantastic, the rainforest green and pristine and the crew on the boat were wonderful and obliging. I should pause here and say that no holiday in Tasmania is complete without a visit to Strahan and the West Coast.

Our stay in Strahan was beyond expectations even though it rained continuously for the two days we stayed there; most unusual the locals said. The cruise was an absolute must do, as we were advised. The part I remember the most was gliding up the Gordon River in the rain, the engines were on idle so there was very little engine noise or vibration. The mist was shrouding the mountains and the whole atmosphere was surreal.

Perhaps this is the reason I get so annoyed when visitors complain about the weather. What the fuck do they expect coming to Tasmania? If they want sun and surf go to Queensland. The climate on the West Coast of Tasmania can be unpredictable at times, but typically bears resemblance to most west coast temperate locations around the world. This is the Roaring Forties bringing with it the weather patterns of the Great Southern Ocean;

periods of liberal rain and the freshest air in the world. Remarkably there are many days of sunshine on the west coast, despite comments from locals in Hobart; and when the sun is shining the days are magic. Let's face it wherever you go there is weather. Why does this come as such a surprise to some people?

It is interesting that I never hear anyone complain about the weather in the South Island of New Zealand. Take Milford Sound for example. Similar weather conditions to the south west of Tasmania so what is it with visitors to Tassie...why are they so obsessed with complaining about the rain when this part of Tasmania has a lot of what many parts of the world would like, moderate rainfall, enough so you don't have to water the garden but not enough to cause floods and disruption.........this is the land of the long hot shower and in Strahan the water through the taps is probably the best you will get anywhere in Australia. Grab your toothbrush and head down to the west coast; it's bloody beautiful mate!

Think about it, if it wasn't for the rain there would be no rainforest, no World Heritage Area, no pristine Gordon and Franklin Rivers. Why is it that some visitors fail to engage their brain before they put their mouth into gear? It's not just the visitors either. There are even some locals down here that insist on talking down what is arguably the best holiday touring destination in Australia, if not the world. Tasmania!

Chapter Seven

'open your wallet and say after me, help yourself'

As we were driving out of Strahan, back in 1995, we checked out an old historic mansion. It just had to have a 'for sale' sign on it and Stephanie, our daughter, reckoned it was a castle and wanted to be princess so Caro and I could be the....; enough. For some unknown and mystical reason, we stopped the car and wrote the agents number down.

We headed off to Stanley and stayed in a charming cottage called Bleak House. Charles Dickens would have been totally at home. The owner had a habit of popping in unannounced through a secret doorway every now and again; at least I think she was the owner. It didn't worry us to any great degree, but it certainly didn't need a ghost; we felt as if it was haunted already. The lady was quite accommodating but a little....err.... different; fucking odd in fact.

Our next stop was at Latrobe and the owner of the guesthouse, Lucinda, was 'absolutely lovely'. We enquired about Ormiston House and she said...............   "You two would be brilliant at running a guesthouse". I am inclined to think it was Mary's fault that we spent all this money; at this stage it all seemed like an adventure. We were cashed up, had some good assets, and life was good. The Paddlewheeler was up for sale. "Let's tip it all into the one bucket and watch it, err.... Disappear."

Important Point: renovating can be very expensive and so is starting a business from scratch. If you are looking at a B & B consider buying an existing business, plan some modest renovations and build it up in stages.

When we got to Launceston my business partner Rob phoned me and told me that someone has made an offer on our cruise business, the Brisbane Paddlewheeler, and would I be happy to go to contract. The price was acceptable, so I said yes. We had previously spoken about selling if the opportunity presented itself.

I put the phone down and said to Carolyn "we have a buyer for the boat".

Over dinner we spoke about what we would do when the boat sold. How about we buy the house (Ormiston) and move to Tasmania? We laughed, "let's just wait a while; this is getting spooky."

By the time we got back to Hobart we spoke to our friends who were excited that we would consider moving to Tasmania. I suggested we speak to the real estate agent, there was a sign on the fence in Strahan and we had jotted down the number. It happened to be an agent in Sorrell not far from where we were staying in Hobart.

The real estate agent was a tall chap with a familiar face. At first glance we could not place it. We asked about the price and who the current owner was. He said the owner was a titled property developer and that if we wished he could arrange an inspection. To head back over to Strahan for an inspection would mean we would need to rearrange part of our holiday. We said we would get back to him.

When we got outside his office I said to our friends "hang on that's the chap in the book we purchased in Strahan

(Through Hell's Gates, by Kerry Pink), The Duke of Avram. The agent is the owner."

We laughed and went back to our friend's place but the whole situation intrigued us. I suggested I call him the next day, front him about who he is and ask for an inspection. We all agreed. The next day, I called and, he admitted that he in fact was the owner and that he would have told us if we proceeded. We arranged an inspection for two days later and we made some changes to our itinerary. Our friends looked after Stephanie for the day and we drove over to Strahan, inspected the property and returned that afternoon a little tired but full of enthusiasm.

During the inspection we took photographs, and a VHS movie as we walked around. I had the 35mm still camera and Carolyn took the VHS movie. The still images turned out OK, but Carolyn had the zoom on the movie camera so all we got were movies of cornices, corners and floorboards. These were the days before digital cameras so we had to wait until we got the 35mm film developed in Brisbane before we could see the images. I of course told Carolyn that she did a great job with the movies and that the intensive close ups of the corners of the rooms would be very useful during the restoration.

During the inspection we poked our heads in the roof cavity and I did see a few drips and a bucket but thought that's Ok, we can deal with that. One bedroom also had a bucket in the middle of the room with a hole in the ceiling and bits of plaster on the floor. Yeah, we can deal with that, not a problem. There was mould and moss on some of the walls. Yeah, we can deal with that. Some cracks in plaster on the walls, not a problem, we can deal with that.

Strangely the house was surprisingly welcoming. Despite the cold and damp, it had a calm atmosphere, almost surreal. Some old houses can be unfriendly and make you feel totally unwelcome, but this house was different. Little did we know that the house was 'actually saying', "Open your wallet and say after me – help yourself". Undaunted we proceeded.

The agent, The Duke, advised us that there was already a contract on the house, however their offer had timed out on the finance, so it really was an opportunity to be first past the post.

Before we left Tasmania and returned to Brisbane, we made an appointment with TDR (Tasmania Development and Resource) as it was known then. One of their functions was to provide statistical information and advice for investment in Tasmania. This was a prudent move and an essential part of any business

plan and to do necessary research. The result was glowing stats on the tourism visitation and potential for investment in Tasmania, including Strahan. We packed up the comprehensive literature

which also included a book on starting a small business in Tasmania. This was looking very good from our perspective.

Chapter Eight

'a sale is not a sale until the money is in the bank'

With our holiday over and the sale of the Paddlewheeler business proceeding well, we decided to do a rough business plan. I recall Carolyn laying all the pictures we took of Ormiston, both internal and external, out on the floor of the family room. At the same time, we played the video of the blurred corners and architraves. At the very least they were giving us some perspective of the layout of the building. We had assets but no ready cash, so I gave a friend a call who was with one of the big banks. With a rough business plan, a few selected photos and the information from TDR we met with my friend, his boss and another loans officer. I won't mention the establishment name as I have a sad story to tell about this bank later. Our assets and liquidity were excellent so bridging finance of $440,000 was agreed upon, mortgage documents signed over on the Bridgeman Downs house and money available for the purchase of Ormiston within the week. One proviso was that we would be selling our major asset at Bridgeman Downs within 12 months which we thought would deal with most of the loan and of course we had the sale of the Paddle Wheeler as well. This was getting too easy.

Then it was crunch time. We had already signed a contract, by fax, with a sunset clause on finance but that was taken care of quickly as the finance came through within a week. We had the money, so we said let's settle. We acquired the services of a Tasmanian solicitor to handle the Tasmania end and do the appropriate title searches and inspect the contract and by the end of April we owned the house in Strahan.

I was getting ready to tell my partner Rob that I may have to head to Tasmania before the contract finalised on the sale of the Paddle Wheeler when he called me at home. "Mike, I've got some bad news. The contract has fallen through. The prick has bought another boat." Apparently, there were some conditional clauses in the contract that I was not aware of that allowed him to opt out before a certain time. "Buggar," I said, "I've just bought a property in Tasmania Rob, I leave in four weeks." Clunk, the phone went dead. In my infinite wisdom I had scheduled our move to Tasmania in line with the anticipated settlement of the Paddle Wheeler sale.

During the working day Rob and I had different duties. I would look after the office and reservations and he would work on the boat doing maintenance and cruise prep. I didn't see or hear from him for 3 days. Finally, he came into the office and we sat down and negotiated an agreement whereby he would run the business and I would forego my profit share as he would need to hire someone to fill my shoes. The boat would remain for sale and upon sale I would get 50% of the proceeds.

Lesson number 1......don't assume a sale is a sale until the money is in the bank.

So, there we were; came to Tasmania for a holiday; bought an historic house in a bad state of repair; restored it and opened a guesthouse and restaurant.

One of my 'Brissy' mates told me I was a 'fucking idiot' but hey, we both just laughed. Many a true word can be spoken in jest.

Carolyn, myself and a friend Valma Pugh who was an interior designer, flew down to Tasmania at the end of April to collect the keys and take a closer look at the house. We arrived in Strahan on a rainy day, most unusual, opened the front door and popped the cork out of a bottle of sparkling wine to toast our new venture. That done I left the girls to measure up and talk about furnishings and colours while I had a close look at what we had purchased.

On the first visit, a few weeks prior, we could see the damaged plaster ceilings, moss and mould in some areas and a few leaks. There were buckets in a couple of rooms and in the roof cavity, however, no problems, my first intention was to replace the roof sheeting and thankfully we already had a contact for that job. How were we to know that tradesmen on the west coast do not advertise in the yellow pages. Why should they? Everyone on the west coast of Tasmania knows who the tradies are; but not if you come from fucking Brisbane mate! This was 1995, no

Google, no internet and buggar, no mobile phone coverage on the West Coast of Tasmania.

As it was raining, I could see how much water was coming in. I emptied the buckets and also observed how much damage was being caused, and had done so for some time; it was really pissing in. I did notice this to some extent on the first visit but perhaps the rain was not particularly heavy that day. As I inspected the roof cavity in detail, I could see that most of the leaks were coming from the 'widows walk' area around the tower. Trouble was that there was a timber deck on top of the old rusted iron roof and the wooden deck would have to be lifted to repair the iron; big job.

I told the girls that the water ingress problem was a little more serious than originally thought but Carolyn suggested I was more than capable of solving the issue. I considered the compliment was more of an actual warning that I did indeed need to find a solution. The female species has a unique way of making their point if we mere males are astute enough to detect the signals. We still had another four weeks before we moved down and started the restoration and a lot of water ingress during that period would just make matters worse.

I decided I would call the local SES and see if they wanted to do some storm damage training. I would donate the house as a training facility if they would leave the tarps on the roof until we got tradesmen on the job. I called the local coordinator who was a miner in the town of Rosebery about fifty kilometres away. I also said I would donate $500.00 to the SES for their assistance. He was extremely happy to have the opportunity to do the training and would do it within a few days and probably during an evening. There is something unique about small remote communities and their willingness to help each other out; something that you don't find in cities and large towns. Of course, the donation helped as emergency services in remote areas are cash strapped and donations are gratefully accepted.

We left Strahan safe with the knowledge that the water ingress would be controlled during our absence over the following four weeks. Carolyn and Thelma were armed with all the measurements required and an understanding of some of the decorating tasks to be tackled.

Chapter Nine

'do not under-estimate the cost of restoring old houses'

We were back in Brisbane, perhaps a few days, when I received a call from the SES in Tasmania. "G'day Mike, got the tarps on but had an accident. One of the guys fell through a skylight. Silly buggar wasn't looking where he was going."

"Geez, is he OK." I knew the skylights in a couple of places were four to five metres high.

"Yeah mate, he'll be OK. He couldn't talk for a while. I'll just have to keep him off roofin' for a bit. His nerves are a bit of a jangle and he's still shaking. I think heights are going to bother him for a while. Anyway, I reckon we've stopped the water getting in. We'll do another exercise after you come down and take the tarps off."

I was glad the chap was all right and called our insurance agent to ensure we had adequate cover for personal damages while the restoration was under way given the amount of roof work to be done. More cost and more cover required. We were lucky.

Lesson number 2....Don't try and save money by not having suitable insurance cover.

We had some money invested in shares, so we converted those to cash and started with a restoration fund of $150,000.... that should be enough.

Lesson number 3 .... do not underestimate the cost of restoring old houses

On return to Brisbane, and during the next four weeks prior to our departure, we planned the restoration.

Carolyn liaised with Valma, the interior designer, and produced a soft furnishing plan for the house which also included procurement of the necessary fabrics, wallpapers, colour schemes and reproduction furniture for the restaurant.

For some strange and unknown reason, we decided that working our arses off seven days a week, three hundred and sixty-five days a year was not going to be enough and we would throw in another 9 hours a day and devote that to a restaurant each evening. It was around this time that I told another friend of mine about our project and he said, "are you fucking mad?" There is something repetitious about the vernacular of Queenslanders when confronted with somewhat humorous scenarios at someone else's expense. We took a long hard look at antique tables and chairs and decided that they were not sufficiently strong enough for big burley miners, so reproduction was the way to go for the restaurant. It was our intention to faithfully integrate the original Edwardian theme in furniture and decor. The house was listed as a building of significant historical interest with local government but at that stage not with the Tasmanian Heritage Council. In fact, the West Coast Local Government Council sent their complete file on the house, by registered mail, to us in Brisbane after I enquired with them as the new owner. Sending such comprehensive documentation would probably not happen today but the general feeling in the community at that time was that we were regarded as "the saviours" of a building that was revered by the local community.

The antique shops in Brisbane thought it was Christmas when we walked in. Our recent experience in Tasmania showed that the antiques at that time were too pricey and the selection was somewhat limited. This was at a time when antiques were in high demand as old houses were getting faithful restorations in all states. We did the rounds of the best that Brisbane had to offer and eventually ended up at a wholesale antique importer in Geebung. Three containers had just arrived from Europe and they were full of French and Belgium wardrobes, English and French dressers and other assorted items. Our intention was to open with three en-suited rooms and within twelve months bring another "two-bedroom" suite online with a bathroom. We purchased, among others, three English dressers c1880, one English wardrobe c1900, two French wardrobes c1890 and one French dresser c1900. I took a fancy to a brass lamp stand with a pigskin shade and an English mahogany roll top desk with bookcase. The inventory was quite comprehensive and no need to go into full detail here, but the images of the rooms on the website show the level to which we aspired to achieve the interior of a stately home at the turn of the 20th century.

The internal doors at Ormiston were traditional four panelled Victorian style and I was not sure at that stage if we would need any extra. It was our plan to close off some doors and create new doorways. Where possible we intended to utilise as much of the original timber jams and architraves in the restoration. I had doubts that anyone close by to Strahan would be able to provide extra period doors of the authentic design at short notice. Together with other period furniture we added four Victorian four panelled doors from one of the restoration shops in Brisbane. The doors in Ormiston, as we later learned were made locally from Huon and King Billy pines. We were also to learn that the faux grain finish on the internal doors would present as a bit of a problem should we wish to replicate or repair the original shellac coatings.

To briefly summarise the departure, the removal truck was booked, the antiques were delivered to our overcrowded garage, the basic restoration plan was finished, colours selected, with fabrics and soft furnishings at some stage of pre-order. I went shopping at Trade Tools and acquired a ute full of new tools, so I was happy. After many phone calls to Tasmania I had organised some trades people to travel to Strahan and give us quotes for various aspects of the restoration. From personal experience, and as a 'more than reasonable' handyman, I was confident that we would be able to do the painting, tiling, basic carpentry and brickwork repair ourselves as well as removal of unwanted materials.

Chapter Ten

'Shit! – what have we done'

During this formative period, we requested our solicitor in Tasmania to register a business name; we suggested Ormiston House. He got back to us a few days later and said there is already an Ormiston Guest House registered for the same address. We asked by whom? He said the name which we recognised as the people who had the previous contract that fell through by way of lack of finance. The bastards had registered as a guest house before they owned the property. We told the solicitor to fix it but a few days later he again contacted us to say that they have refused to hand over the name and legally we cannot force them to cancel the business name without expensive legalities. He advised that they were prepared to sell the name for $2000.00. I was fuming, so angry, in fact very fucking angry. I told him to offer $1000 and thankfully they accepted. The solicitor told us that under the circumstances it was the cheapest option; apparently, they were pissed off that we got the house and they didn't.

The physical part of the journey had begun. Finance was in place. The house at Bridgeman Downs was on the market. The removal truck, a semi-trailer no less, was on its way with our personal effects and the antiques. Our house at Bridgeman Downs was fitted out with contemporary furnishings; at that stage of no use in an historic mansion so we had them put into storage. One of our intermediate plans was to build a new residence at the rear of the mansion for our accommodation. We had a 'five to ten year' plan. Little did we know it would turn out to be 21 years, and here we are, still living in Tasmania today.

In summary, we loved our holiday in Tassie so much that we returned to live following our holiday. The bank virtually threw money at us...they do that when you seem to have a quid but shit, they pull up stumps quickly when they see it disappearing; and we were the proud new owners of a Queen Anne Federation mansion.

There we were. After getting set up very nicely thank you in Brisbane we chucked it all in and moved down to Tasmania. Two cars, two weeks and a rough crossing on Bass Strait and we were driving down the Murchison Highway after a fall of snow. Two and a half Queenslanders thought it was a tad nippy to say the least.

Lill, a girlfriend of Carolyn, came down with us and travelled with her in her car. I was in the other vehicle and I guess she needed someone to talk to; but I did enjoy the calm and quiet of the drive down…. guys know what I mean. In fact, Stephanie joined me in the ute for some of the trip; I guess it was substantially quieter in my car.

The day we arrived we unpacked, had a look around and said "SHIT, what have we done?" "Too late", we said, "so let's do it." After saying to Carolyn "this won't be a problem", "that won't be a problem", "we can fix that", "I can do that". I now said, "we have a problem". Houston, did we have a fucking problem? I told Carolyn I may have underestimated the amount of physical work that we as a couple would have to undertake during the ensuing months. Carolyn said, "Phone Rob Brown". I called Rob Brown, Lill's recently separated partner. Rob worked as a tradies TA and knew his way around building sites. "Rob", I said, "we have a problem; can you spare a month or two?" Rob said he would be down in a few weeks but would be more comfortable if he arrived after Lill went back to Brisbane. We paid for his petrol and Bass Strait ferry fare, promised to have liberal quantities of Bundy rum on hand and waved goodbye to Lill.

My 30th year school reunion in Rockhampton was set for June 6th, 1995 and that, regrettably, was the most convenient day that I could get the tradesmen to come down the west coast to quote on the roof, plumbing and central heating. How did I work that one out... 'buggared if I know?' If I had delayed the start by even a week or two, I had my doubts that we could finish in time for the start of the summer season. So, after a few phone calls I came to the realisation that I had to stay in Strahan, forego the school reunion and get the inspections and quotes sorted. We very quickly learnt that on the west coast of Tasmania, if you get a tradesman on your property then don't 'not be there'. Tradesmen are hard enough to get back to do the job let alone anything else.... hey, that's anywhere, not just Tasmania; if anything, following our experiences, I think they are more reliable down here in Tassie.

The one condition we had, and we put it in writing to all the tradies, was that they had to be on site on the exact day we stipulated. When Carolyn and I planned the restoration, we gave ourselves five months to be open for our first guests. We were spending so much money that we would need the cash flow of the summer season to pay some of the bills. Each stage of the restoration was given a timeline with overlaps of selected specific jobs that would not be 'in conflict' with others. Heating and roof work were the first priorities as the house needed drying out before we could effectively work on the plaster. At the same time the plumbing underfloor, and in the roof space, could be carried out simultaneously without interfering with the other two jobs.

We did have one major problem, as if there weren't enough. All the immediate tradies were from out of town; in fact, not only that, they were from outside of the region. I decided to contact one of our new tourism industry colleagues who owned a cabin park around the corner from our property. I booked two cabins for three months. Whilst we had some spare rooms at our new guesthouse, we did not have any heating, furniture or spare bedding. It was bad enough that 'we' would have to put up with living in a building site; we could not expect tradies to live in those conditions as well.

Besides if I got the tradies to organise accommodation charged back to us it would cost us significantly more.

About two weeks after we arrived the tradies started work so, fortunately, I didn't head back up to Rocky as we would not have got the restoration finished in time. As it was, we gave ourselves five months tops to do a complete restoration. So right on queue the plumber, heating technician and roof Col turned up. What a great crew. Kurt was the young plumber just out of his apprenticeship, his mate Mark from the same firm doing the central heating and Roof Col. Then there were Carolyn, Rob, me and Ground Col, who would arrive shortly.

One day Roof Col got the shock of his life when I met him on the roof with a silver tray, Royal Doulton china, English breakfast tea and a nice hot scone. "Afternoon tea, squire," I said. He nearly fell off the roof. You would never get a tradie anywhere else but Tassie to work in these rough west coast conditions. Col took a couple of tumbles and one time we saw him lying flat face down on a 50-degree roof slope and I swear his fingernails had cut into the roofing iron as he slid down. No safety harness, no scaffolding but that was how the older tradies worked backed then. At times when it was raining Roof Col would throw a tarp over himself, and the hole in the roof, and keep working.

One day another chap called around. His name was Colin also. He asked us if we needed someone to do odd jobs, any jobs. Ground Col was a fisherman on dry land. His wife

Joyce had the fish and chip van on the Strahan wharf, and I tell you, they had the best fish and chips I have ever tasted and simply the best battered Tassie scallops. Joycey, Ground Col's wife, was also a great artist. Col used to organise the fish and get in Joyce's way when she was cooking so she would send him around to our place to make himself useful but during the evenings she would relent and allow Col to give her a hand in the van. Ground Col was one of those blokes who could lend himself to most things. He was a great bush carpenter and could do anything with wood. Col was also mild mannered however one day the seaplane owner in the adjacent building tried to get the fish van moved off the wharf. An altercation ensued and it was then that we realised that Col was also good with his fists.

Painting was another job we gave Ground Col. In fact, we all did the painting, but Ground Col was colour blind. He had red green confusion which worked out a bit tricky seeing as we had green gutters and a red roof. When Ground Col spilt green paint on the red roof, he couldn't see it. I went up there one day towards the end of the restoration and there was green paint all over the roof. "Fuckin' hell Col what's all this." He couldn't see it until he ran his fingers over the wet paint. I asked him how he got his skippers ticket for the fishing boat if he had red green confusion. He just winked at me and I knew better than to push for an answer.

Chapter Eleven

'do ghosts eat chocolate?'

After Carolyn's girlfriend, Lill, went home her husband Rob arrived and worked with us for about 4 months. They were in the process of splitting up so we couldn't have them both down here at the same time. Funny that.

Rob brought down his ute, 'chock a block' with tools and together with everything I had we could've opened a Bunnings Store. Locals still came to see me years later in case I had some bits or pieces as I used to have more stuff here than the local hardware store. As I previously mentioned Rob used to do some jobbing work as a tradie's assistant, so he knew his way around a building project and was as strong as an ox. At first, he thought I was his tradie's assistant until we got that sorted.

It had been my intention to make some super neat cuts in the internal brickwork for where we had intended to create new doorways. To this end I had purchased a petrol driven, handheld, masonry diamond saw. A bit like a chain saw with a circular blade instead of a chain. It also had a water-cooled kit that fitted to the cowling over the blade to keep the blade from over-heating. I assessed that this would make a bit of a mess so I got the plumbing firm to make a metal tray that I could stand in while cutting through the brickwork and which would also collect the water. This would minimise the water and mess on the internal wooden floor. Talk about a trap for young players. For a start the water pissed out everywhere and the fumes from the petrol motor soon filled up the room. To add to this disaster in motion as soon as the blade cut through the render and plaster, and contacted with the bricks, instead of cutting through the brick, the bricks started moving and shuddering. The masonry saw was then put back into the storeroom and the metal tray was banished to the garden and used as a dog bath. For the rest of the restoration internal brickwork was removed one brick at a time and might I add, very carefully.

Work routines were established quickly. We would all start early, then Caro would organise breakfast, then lunch and we would all knock off around 5pm. This was a Tassie winter; dark 'til 7am and dark again at 5pm. Then it was into the old kitchen, which we were also in the process of pulling apart, and break out the scotch, rum and brandy and all have a few drinks before Caro would knock up some dinner. Kurt, Mark and Roof Col were staying at the cabin park just down the road and frequently would stay for dinner. Ground Col would usually knock off at around 4pm and go back to the van on the wharf and start filleting the fish for the evening rush and annoying Joycey.

More than likely it would be raining day and night. On the occasions when the weather cleared, we would then have frosts to contend with. If we were lucky, we would get a bit of sunshine. Shortly after Ground Coll arrived, I organised a truck load of timber and roof trusses for a nine metre by nine metre timber framed carport. Initially the main reason for that was to have somewhere dry where we could store all the materials and equipment that was arriving, almost daily. Between Ground Col, Rob and myself we had it erected in a couple of days and at last we had outside storage and could work outside, undercover, when it was raining.

Caro and I set up our bedroom in one of the large dining rooms that was minimally damaged by water ingress, with Steph in the room next to us. Rob was down the end of the east west passage in what is now the Christina room. Some of the rooms were just too badly damaged for us to live comfortably in.

One of the first things we did internally was to rip up the old cherry red shagpile carpet. Ground Col reckoned it would look extremely good in his shack up at Montague, so we gave that to him. Then while roof Col was going one for one on the roof, young Mark was bashing and crashing in the roof space installing the heating and ducting so he and Roof Col would be chatting away through the holes in the roof.

Kurt was busy in the roof and under the floors with the plumbing and Rob and I were busy cutting holes in the floors and making gaps in the footings so we could move around under the house. Given there was only about 60cm clearance she was a bit of a squeeze in places. I was a bit slimmer in those days.

One night we had cleaned up from dinner, the tradies had gone back to their cabins and we went to bed. By this time our little miniature silky terrier Tiffany had arrived from Queensland. Gorgeous little dog, although our daughters thought she was a nasty piece of work. She was in a basket near our door (Tiffany, not our daughter), and the sliding doors between our room and Stephanie's room were pulled closed but just a small gap so we

could check she was all right. Stephanie was 5 years old and quite the little lady.

About 2am Tiffany starts growling. I wake up and look down the passageway…. this is a big house and the passageways are huge, but nothing visible. The silky takes off and runs down the passageway stopping outside Rob's room and has a growl. I have a look around the place but don't see anything, so I go back to our bedroom, tell the dog its stupid, check on Steph, who is in bed, and so I turn in.

The next morning, we find that a half-eaten block of chocolate on the kitchen table is missing. Do ghosts eat chocolate? I think not.

The next night the same thing happens but this time I walk all the way around the house and once again the chocolate (we kept Cadburys going that winter) is missing. By the time I get back to our room all is quiet, Steph is in bed, so

I turn in and tell the dog it's not so stupid and something is going on.

The next morning Rob is as white as a sheet and tells us that the house is haunted and that there was a ghost in his room. Big brave Rob was shivering under the sheets as this bright light danced around the room in the middle of the night and he didn't sleep at all after the incident.

The next night Tiffany and I were ready - ghost busters. I left the chocolate out as usual in the kitchen.

At around 2am the dog growls but instead of going down the passageway we headed straight for the kitchen to find Stephanie helping herself to the chocolate then comes the confession.

The previous night when Tiffany and I headed down the passageway she ducked into Rob's bedroom after she picked up the chocolate and turned her torch on as she hid in the room. Rob thought the torch light was a ghost and hid under the bed clothes. When Tiff and I raced off to the kitchen to find the chocolate gone Steph raced back to her bedroom and pretended to be asleep.

So, the mystery was solved. The dog got a pat and the kid didn't get any more chocolate at 2am. Rob's still scared of ghosts.

Talking of ghosts. When we moved here the sister at the medical centre told us that the house was haunted by a lady in a grey dress who could be seen in the attic and tower. I am a bit of a believer but as mentioned our silky terrier never gave any indication that there was anything amiss. The restoration was totally ghost free apart from the odd feelings that you were not alone in the room at times. However, one day something strange did happen.

About three months into the restoration, so about the end of August I think, we had to finish some external painting as the town promotion group was putting together a brochure and was taking photographs of the accommodation properties. In those days there were about ten accommodation properties. Today there are about 40. If anyone has been on the west coast of Tasmania for any length of time, they would know that it gets a fair amount of its annual rainfall in winter. During the restoration we let the weather dictate our activity. If it was a fine day we worked outside and if it was raining, we worked inside. By doing it this way we could ensure that we got all the jobs done within our schedule. Well that was the plan and it worked most of the time except when the rain persisted, and we needed to finish an external job.

So it was, as the deadline approached, that we had to finish the gutters and wrought iron lacework around the verandas. There we were on trestles, ladders and milk crates, all four of us, racing against the weather and the clock. We were nearly finished on this one day. It had been cloudy, and we had about 10 metres of veranda to go. It was late afternoon and we knew that if the weather held out that we could get the job finished as the forecast the next day was not good. Then the rain started spitting and so did Carolyn. She looked up into the sky and, in a pleading voice, called on the last three Frederick Ormiston Henrys (they were deceased by the way) for a bit of help and co-operation. Carolyn did not swear much in those days. Under my breath I was saying "for fuck's sake you guys, give us a fucking break". Almost immediately the rain spits stopped and within a few minutes a patch of blue sky appeared which stayed with us until we finished the last section of veranda. No sooner had we finished than the light rain started again. We did end up with a few water spot marks on the gutters but that was about it and we fixed them up later in the year. The important aspect was that we had the right colour up there for the photographs a couple of days later. We thought that was a little spooky, but we thanked the 'Freds' in any case. I apologised for my cussing and to this day we don't know if they were listening to Carolyn or me.

Chapter Twelve

'F O Henry's gold would come in handy'

While Roof Col was busy taking one old sheet of iron off and putting another new one on the four of us, Rob, Ground Col,

Caro and myself decided that we needed to get the widows walk pulled apart and the deck lifted up so that Roof Col could replace the iron sheeting with the new colour bond roofing. This was all very well in theory however the weather was so unpredictable. The only thing predictable about Strahan in winter is that it most definitely may or may not rain. I made a drawing of the deck and balustrading and we started by removing the ironwork first. It was original cast iron and extremely heavy. We needed to store it in the undercover area and so it had to be carried down three flights of stairs, piece by piece. To avoid damaging the timber railings many of the old rusty screws had to be cut out with a hacksaw. That done the railings had to be removed. The corners were mortice and tenon. Some were in reasonable shape and testament to the durability of Huon and celery top pine. Others were rotten and despite its reputation Huon pine will rot over time once the natural oil in the timber has weathered away. Each rail was numbered and noted on the drawing so that we would be able to replace in the same position once the roof had been repaired. The deck of the Widows Walk was a floating frame pinned into the base of the tower. There was a slope in the deck away from the tower to allow for run off with each piece of timber decking cut exactly to the slope and many angles involved. We numbered each piece of decking in addition to the posts and railings. All pieces were then stored in the under-cover area. Once the decking was removed, we then had to put tarps over the roof framework.

The roof was constructed using Tasmanian A grade eucalypt. In Tasmania it is known as Tassie oak but is a variety named Mountain Ash. The correct name is *eucalyptus regnans.* The same variety in Victoria is known as Victorian Ash. Roof Col, surprisingly, only found one purlin that needed to be replaced while he was working on the roof. Fortunately, I had already ordered a bundle of Tassie oak to have on hand for such contingencies. Such is the durability, as I have already mentioned, of Tasmanian timber.

On some mornings we would come to the roof to start work on the widows walk area and the water pooled in the tarps would be frozen and we would have to crack the ice to get the tarps off and without allowing any water to enter the roof cavity. It was with great relief when Roof Col got the area re-sheeted and we could get the deck back in place. Getting the deck back in place was not so arduous as we had the plan and numbered parts. However, the posts, railings and iron work were an entirely different matter. The external temperatures were so low that the paint would not dry outside. I had decided to use oil-based enamels for the external and internal trim. These were all full gloss enamels and would provide an excellent finish with colours in keeping with the federation theme. However, with temperatures under ten degrees Celsius, the paint would take an indeterminable time to dry and harden. Skinning off was not good enough the paint had to be hard as well as dry.

As the bar area would be one of the last rooms to be finished, I decided to use that room as a drying room for the posts, rails and iron work. Mark was nearly finished installing the central heating which would be powered by LPG. The assessment initially had indicated that LPG would be the cheapest way to go. I contacted the gas supplier and we got four cylinders linked and plumbed in by Mark and we were finally ready to start heating the house up. In turn this would also dry the plaster and internals and we could start on the walls and ceilings.

We turned the gas on and ran the gas for six weeks day and night before the internal of the house was ready to work on. The first four cylinders ran out quickly and a three-tonne gas tank was installed. During that first year, '95/'96 we chewed up $15,000 of LPG. We were not expecting that. That expenditure continued for another five years.

Sadly, the last and third, F O Henry passed away early in our restoration, but we were fortunate to get to know him. He was certainly pleased that at last someone was going to spend some money on restoring his old house to its former glory. The story of the Henry family is very much part of the history of Ormiston House and I would recommend reading The Ormiston House Book if you are interested.

It was with some sadness when we said goodbye to Roof Col, Kurt and Mark however we were to meet up with them all again as the years passed by. Roof Col went back to Hobart and Mark back to Burnie leaving one cabin vacant. Kurt eventually returned to Burnie but one day, sitting in the kitchen after toiling under the floors of Ormiston, we had a delivery of some ocean trout from one of the fish farms. The delivery was undertaken by a tall, attractive blond girl called Susan; the daughter of the fish farm owner. They are now married with a lovely family and Kurt now has his own plumbing business based in Strahan. Mark and Kurt were to return a little later in the restoration to apply some finishing touches to their excellent work.

Kurt, Mark and Roof Col's cabins in the park were not vacant for very long before the plasterers arrived from Ulverstone. After a summary inspection the senior of the two tradies remarked "you could probably spend the rest of your lives working on the plaster problems." They immediately got to work repairing and replacing the three worst ceilings. The bar area was considered repairable so that was strapped up with steel into the rafters pulling the old lath and plaster back up into position whereby they then re-sheeted with plasterboard. One of the bedrooms had already been repaired with Masonite board, with the original lath and plaster removed some years ago; re sheeting would be quite simple. The old sitting room which was to be our office was also strapped and covered with plasterboard. It was then onto the cracks and fissures in the rendered walls.

The internal walls of Ormiston were three bricks thick. Interlocking British brick pattern with a lime mortar which was soft and crumbly in many places. Drying the house out had certainly helped but some areas were very brittle indeed. The senior plasterer sat me down and said, "let's talk." As he had previously mentioned we could spend the rest of our lives making the plaster looking as near new as we could. However, in his view, and very quickly mine, this was not a new house and the aged plaster was in fact part of the character of the house. His opinion was that while they would repair the major defects, they would need to ensure that the finish would have to blend in with the old surface otherwise we would either need to completely re-finish every surface or have smooth shiny patches intermittingly visible upon the older rougher original plaster. The render on the internal brickwork varied in thickness obviously with the original plasterers ensuring all vertical surface were true. The render they used was made from the existing sand the house was built on, lime mortar and using horsehair as a binder. Within the render were crushed seashells and in some cases the shells were intact. Also, in amongst the sandy render were gold coloured pyrites, also known as fool's gold. There was an old local rumour that the original F O Henry had buried his gold within the house somewhere. I found evidence during our restoration that previous owners had indeed been excavating under the floor spaces, perhaps looking for buried treasure. I could not help but think that a bit of the original F O Henry's gold would come in handy to pay for this fucking restoration.

It was decided that the plasterers would do their best to blend the new with the old and they did in fact do a splendid job. They could not however spend the rest of their lives working on the plaster but I, apparently, could. I did a fast apprenticeship of plastering while they were in situ for three weeks and it was to be my job to repair the lesser of the plaster damage. Not long after they departed I was removing a door jam, to make room for a heating return air duct, when a nail I had failed to notice caught behind some old render and as I pulled it away from the area it caused over a square metre of old render to fall away from the wall in the passageway. Shit! I now had a huge hole to fill but thankfully I had acquired the necessary skills to fix the job. However, it took a few days to repair the damage that I had not planned for. Progressively the remainder of the plaster and render were repaired together with many minor disasters and expletives.

Of course, during the restoration there were many times when we re-assessed our schedules and of course had to leave the house to shop around, so to speak. Carolyn had planned the arrival of restaurant furniture, fabrics, wallpapers and other bits and pieces. There was tapware, basins, baths and electrical switches and plugs to be sourced and purchased. We also had to purchase tiles for the bathrooms.

Now that we were into the internal restoration in earnest, I could accurately measure and assess the amount of tiling necessary. Carolyn had chosen the style and colour of tiles required and having recently built a new house had some idea of the cost. Carolyn used that experience to rough cost the tiles required. I was now assigned to the task of allocating the exact amount required. Armed with drawings, swatches and samples Carolyn and I visited two tiling retailers in Tasmania. One of the tiles was a federation wall tile which Carolyn had assessed as being around $25.00 per square metre. The first retailer we went to had them in stock for $46.00 per square metre. The second retailer was at a similar price. On further inspection Carolyn assessed that the tiles were going to cost close to double what she had thought. We decided to go back to Ormiston and rethink the tile thing.

I went to the local post office and got a copy of the Melbourne yellow pages. Remember, no internet, no Google. I then phoned a tile company in Melbourne. The same Federation wall tile we had looked at in Launceston for $46.00 per square metre was $18.00 per square metre but if we were buying in quantity it would be $16.00 per square metre. I told him that there would be a significant order and he agreed to give us his very best price. I then called one of the local tile retailers and asked him to reconfirm the tile price. He confirmed $46.00. I said I can get it in Melbourne for $16.00. He said, "but you will have to pay freight across Bass Strait." I said, "what for $30.00 a square metre." Then he just hung up on me. I didn't even have time to tell him to get fucked.

The price differences did not stop there. Carolyn and I put together the tile order together with the required quantity of adhesives and grout and gave it to the retailer in Melbourne. I asked him to give me a detailed quote and to provide the weight and pallet size so I could get an idea of freight costs. He agreed and said that when I get the freight quote let him know as he knew a company that would ship to Tasmania. The next day we get the quote and it would be on one and a half pallets. I recall that the weight was around 1250 kg.

I called a Tasmanian freight company and got a quote of $1500.00 to cart from the retailer in Melbourne to Strahan. I thought that was a bit steep, so I called the tile retailer in Melbourne. He gave me the number of his contact. Their quote for delivery to Strahan was $355.00. I, of course, accepted the quote immediately. I looked at Carolyn and said you will never guess the difference in the quotes. We were gobsmacked. About ten days later the tiles arrived delivered by the same Tasmanian freight company that wanted to charge us $1500.00. I rest my case. Who do you think was going to pocket the difference? Bastards. Both Caro and I were incensed and spread the word wherever we could. Most Tasmanians would not believe us. It wasn't until Harvey Norman came to Tasmania that whitegoods and other home furnishings also came down in price. One of our early houseguests, who was an executive for a mainland grocery product manufacturer, told us back in 1997 that Coles and Woolworths in Tasmania were the company's most profitable stores. In those days they operated under different names. We soon found out that the major food retailers also controlled the local food wholesalers who supplied the smaller independent grocery stores and other businesses as well; companies that would be some of our suppliers in our restaurant. Thankfully times have changed, and Tasmania enjoys better retail prices than twenty-five years ago.

Chapter Thirteen

'another trip to the bank'

After the tile exercise ended favourably, I suddenly realised I had forgotten an essential part of the restoration; the electrical upgrades. We had been in Tasmania for about 8 weeks when it suddenly dawned on me; I had forgotten to factor in the cost of electrical work. Fuck, in fact multiple fucks. I was experiencing my first 'clusterfuck'. Strahan had a couple of ageing electricians but great guys who knew their stuff. We had to get two new switch boards and a heap of re-wiring before we got to the stage of finishing off the plaster repair and painting. We also had external wiring on the verandas to do and I wanted driveway lights as well. Oh Shit! We haven't even got a driveway yet. Could this be a double clusterfuck?

Thankfully Clem, the electrician, was a local and was happy to come and go as we needed him. The pressure was off; he would work with us and fit in when needed. He did say "I was wondering when you were going to call me".

It was time to call the earth moving guys and get a rough driveway in the front of the house and some trenches for pipes and cables.

Time was marching on and we were starting to get the internals in better shape. Ground Col was working around the outside of the house doing odd jobs. Joyce, his wife, had been sitting in the front garden on fine days while we were finishing off and had painted a picture of the house which we have kept to this day. Rob and I were getting the bathrooms prepped. Kurt had brought the services up through the floor and up the walls. There was a massive wardrobe in the master bedroom which thankfully was a skilfully constructed antique. We found the hidden screws and disassembled it into five sections and stacked it in the passageway together with mantles, over-mantles, compressors, saws and other assorted items.

We had decided to name the three bedrooms after three members of the original Henry family; F O Henry, Mary Alice and Amelia. There was a room in the attic where we had decided to have a small museum and called it the Harry Lyell History Gallery after the youngest son of F O Henry, who was tragically killed in WW1. It was time for another shopping trip to get some brassware, nameplates for the doors and hardware for the fireplaces. We called Mark back in to install gas burners in the old Victorian coal grates to add a sense of realism and a little warmth to the front rooms where we would have the dining rooms, bar and breakfast rooms. It was not practical to burn wood as we found out that the grates were too small, and the chimney casings leaked smoke into the roof cavity.

I had repaired the cracks and water stains in the ceilings, and it was now time to start painting the ceilings before the wallpaper and carpet guys arrived. Time was not our friend. We had reached the stage of Carolyn, Rob and I working until late evening most nights getting odd jobs done after the tradesmen had gone home. We had rebooked the cabin park so that the wallpaper and carpet guys had somewhere to stay.

The trenching had just been completed and thankfully no plumbing installed in the trenches when a removal truck arrived with more antiques and reproduction furniture from Brisbane. The driveway at the front was not completed and there were still trees to be pruned. The side of the house had trenches dug for new power and water pipes. The furniture had to come through the front door, so the removalists had to carry the furniture, including an antique piano, along the veranda to the front of the house. After a couple of movements, the removalists lost their cool and against my advice decided to move the truck down the side of the house closer to the front door. I said watch out for the trenches. Too late the back wheels slid into a trench and the truck leaned over and tilted to within a few centimetres of the veranda awning. The truck tried moving forward but dug in even deeper; the whole of our property is just sand. I made a quick call to the earth moving contractor who brought an excavator around and pulled the truck out and back to its original position. The remainder of the furniture was then carried down the veranda by two red faced removalists with Carolyn giving them advice along the way. She does that very well.

One of the articles delivered was an old piano that we purchased just before we left Brisbane. We bought it off a lady who told us that it used to belong to her grandfather who purchased it as an engagement gift for his bride to be. They both played the piano and subsequently married. He went off to World War One as an ambulance driver and medic. He returned from the war, however by this time he was a heavy smoker and he would play the piano with his head stooped and a cigarette continually in his mouth blowing the smoke over the keys. This was the reason, apparently, that the keys in the middle of the keyboard were stained a yellow brown colour. Shortly after we arrived the school across the road had a visiting piano tuner, so I paid him to look at our piano as it was very out of tune. He told us the sad news that the piano had a timber frame and to make matters worse there was a split in the timber that held the pins. Being the 'eternal optimist' I was happy to leave the piano in the bar area as it was a lovely looking antique Chappell with elaborate sconces. I was equally happy that once a guest played a few notes they would leave it alone and we would not have to tolerate hours upon hours of very average piano playing by guests with an over inflated opinion of their musical prowess.

Around this time one of us said "what are we going to put on the walls?" This was something we had noted but had not actioned. Carolyn asked around and a name was given to us. Within a few days a gentleman called, holding a quantity of catalogues and frame samples. He left shaking a couple of hours later with 46 prints to frame and an order of around $12,000.00; all limited edition and covering rural, classic and maritime themes sympathetic to our federation restoration. I also requested an assortment of frames so that not all pictures looked like they were framed on the same day by the same framer. We wanted artwork to reflect the style of paintings that may have been hanging on the walls of Ormiston at the turn of the century (1900). We would have loved to have original artworks, oils and watercolours but the budget was not that big. We had already blown the budget and gone to the bank for another $50,000.

When Carolyn had contacted the carpet manufacturer for an order, we were told we had to go through their Tasmanian distributer. Here we go again we thought. We had no choice; Carolyn had chosen the carpet and the remainder of the interior decor was based around the carpet colour; we proceeded. We were then advised by the carpet distributer that there was not enough stock available until the end of the year. Shit! We were opening on the 1st November. We asked what we could do? The distributer got back to us and said that due to the importance of our restoration the manufacturer was happy for us to jump the queue, but we would have to pay in advance for the order. Well, that took care of $54,000.00 and hence another trip to the bank as that cleaned us out ahead of schedule. We now had enough money in the bank to get us to opening day; or so we thought.

With some of the painting done and working outside when the sun was shining and inside when it rained, we were working towards our deadline.

Chapter Fourteen

'Rob had a look of horror on his face'

Initially our soft opening was going to be 1st October, with a 'buggar factor' of 30 days. The 'buggar factor' was soon consumed; we were now working towards an opening on 31st October 1995.

The wallpaper hangers had started and were doing a brilliant job. The rooms were really looking exactly as planned. The carpet layer had arrived and was a young chap called Andrew who excelled in laying federation style carpets. Carolyn had chosen a border and matching main carpet in an Axminster. Andrew started and was a consummate professional in every respect. Around this time Carolyn, Rob and I were recovering from copious tiling and painting when I noticed some spring in the front room floors. I was not overly concerned as I thought a bit of chocking was all that was required however Andrew was making good progress following the wallpaper guys from room to room. He was taking around one and a half days per room and had already finished the 'east west' and 'north south' hallways. I said to Rob that I'd better get down below and see what needs to be done before Andrew catches up. Mark was the only one who had been down below in the front rooms when he had installed the gas units in the fireplaces. When he did those installations, he used a manhole in the passageway but that was now sealed and covered with carpet. Shit, here we go again. Rob and I cut a hole in the first dining room and under I went. To my dismay the spring in the floor was caused by the support posts under the bearers having rotted away so it was just the bearers with no support holding up the floor. The bearers were resting on the brick ledges around the room and thankfully they were of significant size to hold the weight however there was some spring in the span and we needed to insert new posts. Andrew however was only one room behind us. Thankfully the wallpaper hangers were in the bar area as the first two dining rooms were painted. I told Rob to start cutting up some of the old Huon pine fence posts that we had stacked up in the yard. We had salvaged then some time ago and were awaiting some use. They were four inches square in the old imperial measurement and, being Huon Pine, they were easy to cut but also would not rot. Ideally, I would have liked to have put concrete posts in, but we were out of time and with only a couple of weeks to go for opening we did not have any choice.

So, the much slimmer me in those days was under the floor yelling up measurements to Rob who was cutting sections and passing them down to me. I had the framing nail gun and was placing a Huon pine section on the sand and one vertical thumped into position to take the weight of the floor and nailed both ends. We did this alongside every rotted post under the four front rooms. Thankfully the timber lasted the job and we stayed just ahead of Andrew and put the manhole back in place in the last room as he was about to lay the carpet.

More scotch, brandy and rum those nights seemed to do the trick.

While all this was happening, we had to have the centre panel in the front door re-leaded. The stained glass was in reasonable condition except for the door so we got a local guy called Steve in to remove it. I decided it needed some finesse and half-way through the restoration I was over finesse. Steve removed it and we sent it away to 'Lady in Lead' on the north coast. I also got Steve to do some other jobs that I would not have time to do. One was the wine racks in the cellar. This was originally a cupboard under the stairs where we removed the floor, scarfed out around the footings and used the bricks from doorways we created and where Ground Col laid some steps and a floor for the cellar. Another job Steve did was replace a few cracked windows and create small flyscreens that slot in under the sash windows. He was also on hand after we lifted the new oven into the kitchen as the window broke as we were putting it back. The oven was too big to get through the doorway. Shit happens.

I have to say that we had a great crew on the restoration, and it proceeded, for the most part, with military precision. We did our bit for the Tasmanian economy and spread the dollars around. Andrew the carpet layer was from

Devonport, the plasterers from Ulverstone, Darryl the wallpaper and painter from Launceston, Roof Col from Hobart and Kurt and Mark from Burnie and Clem the electrician in Strahan.

As the restoration came to a closure, we needed to have some staff employed. On a recent evening out at what was then the Strahan Motor Inn we noticed the receptionist. A pretty, vivacious girl whom we both commented on as just the type of person we needed for Ormiston House.

We were knocked over a couple of weeks later when Jodi turned up on our doorstep and asked if we needed any staff. In fact, we were looking for a house manager and a chef. We literally fell over ourselves to welcome her. What a coup. As it turned out Jodi really was the pick of the hospitality pool in Strahan.

No sooner had we said "yes" than she came back in her work clothes, picked up a paintbrush and said, "where do I start." We were also joined by Karen, the niece of the nursing sister at the clinic next door who was looking for casual waitressing work who also was happy to help with painting and cleaning.

When it came to locating a chef Jodi said, "I know a chef who has resigned from a pub and is leaving the west coast." She promptly got in her car and drove around town until she found him. She came back and said, "he'll be here this afternoon for an interview."

And so it was that the crew fell into our laps, helped us with the final stages of the restoration and became part of the Ormiston House story. We opened with three rooms for guests with 'en-suites', a commercial kitchen and a restaurant for house guests called 'Fredericks'.

The last day of the restoration we worked until 3am finishing off the rooms. We had to install some lath boards and hang the last of the curtains. It was around 2.30am and we were in the bay window of dining room one. Rob was on top of the ladder and I was passing up the lath board for him to fasten. Carolyn was standing by with the curtain rails. As Rob was screwing in one of the brackets his cordless drill fell out of his hands. Caro and I had our hands full. Rob had a look of horror on his face as we watched the drill dropping to the carpet. It had 2 ways to go when it hit the carpet. Fall back into the room or fall into the 'full length' window. It fell against the 'full length' window and the whole glass fell to pieces. We stood there aghast. This was singly the biggest window section in the house and part of a two-piece sash window come doorway. It was an original piece of glass, typical of old cylinder glass with ripples and imperfections. We called it a night after I taped some plastic sheeting over the space. We would have to live with it. I called Steve the next day, but it would be three weeks before he could replace it due to its size. Rob was inconsolable that he had caused the accident. Shit happened again mate, don't sweat it.

Chapter Fifteen

'cold showers and no mirror'

We decided, stupidly, that our first guests would be three travel writers. Dumb; in fact, dumber than dumb. In fact, it was not our idea originally. We employed a media advisor and he suggested it, so we went with the idea, with somewhat trepidation. Carolyn and I had originally planned to stay a few nights in each of the rooms to test them out. Why didn't we do that? For one thing we ran out of time and for another Carolyn did not want to mess the rooms up, just for us...at that late stage it seemed selfish in some way. We had contacted the Strahan Primary School P & F and suggested that they manage an open day on the 31st October so that the folks in town could view the house. You see Ormiston House was one of those stately homes that, being owned by what you would call the aristocracy of the town, hardly anyone had been inside, with the exception of personal friends of the owners and perhaps school friends of the children that lived there.

Early that day we laid down strips of carpet protector and put some small chain across the doorways so that the bedrooms did not get messed up or the carpets marked by dirty feet. Suddenly someone asked where the paintings were. Buggar! We had completely forgotten to hang the artwork we had delivered a few days before. There were over forty framed limited edition prints somewhere. They were in the breakfast room and we had forgotten about that room as well. We removed the framed prints and locked the door; time to worry about that room later.

So, what Carolyn suggested was that we just place them around the passageways in the location that they will be hanging so at least the visitors would see the style of artwork. When the P & F opened the house, the townsfolk shuffled through and some of them commented on the fact that the framed artwork was on the floor. Carolyn heard this and told them that was what we did in Queensland as it was easier to move them around the house for a bit of a change every now and then. Carolyn of course was joking but some of them took it seriously. A few months later one of the dinner guests remarked to Carolyn, "Oh I see you decided to hang the prints on the wall instead of leaving them on the floor." No comment.

While the open day was underway, I headed off to Burnie Airport to pick up two of the journalists from the mainland who were flying in just after midday. Because Carolyn's car was small, and my work ute was not quite up to it, I had arranged for a hire car to bring them down to Strahan and return them two days later. I arrived after the open day was over and the third journalist from Hobart checked in not too long after that.

As it turned out the open day was a roaring success including our novel way of displaying framed artwork. Jodi, our house manager, knew everyone in town so she took charge. The school made over $1000 dollars in gold coin admissions and all were happy.

The first evening with the journalists was perfect. Dinner in house cooked by Rob our chef who was doing a pretty good job. We didn't ask for anything fancy. Just good food, good produce and well presented.

The next morning just before breakfast one of the journalists asked me if he could use the bathroom of one of the other journalists. When I asked why he said the water was not very hot. "Buggar", I thought. Not what we really want on the first day and with a journalist as well.

When I approached the second journalist, he said "not a problem," but he had a cold shower as the hot water did not seem to be working. Double buggar; not really what I wanted to hear. The third journalist confirmed our worst fears.

I headed up to the roof and checked out the hot water systems and they were all hot and the pipes were as well. What could be wrong? Our own bathroom was on a different system and was working well.

I immediately phoned the plumbers in Burnie and Kurt was quickly dispatched down to Strahan, a two-hour drive. In the meantime, the journalists either had a cold shower (Tassie cold) or none, and thankfully a filling breakfast, then sent to do some tourism around Strahan and a scenic flight on one of the seaplanes.

Kurt arrived and quickly set about finding out what was wrong with the hot water. He checked out the valves and pipes before concluding that the new water main carrying the cold water into the house was at such a pressure that the mixing valves carrying the hot water at a less pressure were not opening fully. In my infinite wisdom I had got Kurt to put in a ring main around the house the same diameter as the main water pipe in the street.

Being Strahan there were not enough reducing valves in stock so Kurt had to ring Burnie to get someone to bring three reducing valves so the journalists could have a hot shower when they got back from a day's touring.

In the meantime, Rob Brown and I were busy hanging the framed artwork when Carolyn comes in and says I have just found the bathroom mirror for the F O Henry room. "What?" we said. There was a look of displeasure from Carolyn. "Guys, no mirror in the F O Henry bathroom, you didn't put it in."

Fuck! Rob and I stop with the artwork and then fix the mirror to the wall in the FO Henry room. Then back onto the wall art. Ground Col had since gone back fishing, so it was just Rob and I on maintenance. At this stage I was pretty pissed off because the picture frames were all identical and not the mix of three designs that I had ordered.

When the journalists returned, we had hot water to the rooms and most of the artwork up. The picture hanging was slowed down by the fact that some of the bricks came loose as we were hammer drilling the fasteners into the brickwork behind the old render and plaster. Sometimes it would take two or three holes to find a good hold.

One of the journalists came out of his room shortly after arriving back and said "I love this place. Every time I go out and come back there is something different. When I had a shave this morning, I used the mirror on the dressing table, when I come back there is a new mirror in the bathroom." He laughed; we felt sick.

I drove them back a day later and when I returned, the guy from Hobart, the one who welcomed the new shaving mirror, was still in the house having wine and cheese on the widows walk.

Chapter Sixteen

'to boldly go where no other guesthouse has gone'

That night we welcomed our first paying house guest. He was a trout fisherman and during his visit he caught a trout at Lake Burbury nearby, proudly brought it back and the chef cooked and served it up as an entrée for the three house guests.

I recall several events on the night; the trout which I had already mentioned; one couple who were also B & B owners from Burnie who, during their visit, managed to pull the curtains down in their room; the other couple were from Smithton in the north west of Tasmania.

I had an old brass bugle on the mantelpiece in the bar and the man from Smithton said that looks old. I stupidly said if anyone can play the last post, they can have any drink they want from the top shelf, on the house. He promptly grabbed the bugle and played the last post. He had been in the army years before as a bugler. That was the last time I made that offer. The funny thing was that when he started to play, the other house guests thought that was how we called everyone to dinner. So, they raced out into the bar, thinking they were late.

The bugle is still with us today. Unlike the antique brass master mariners telescope that was also on the mantelpiece, that about fifteen years ago someone decided to take with them when they left. I have a feeling that anyone who has stolen something from Ormiston House may have grave misfortune. That's my theory and I feel good knowing that karma just might catch up with any perpetrators.

I can still remember some of our original houseguests from fifteen years ago. There was a couple from North Scotland at Thurso, whom we thoroughly enjoyed the company of. In those days we started off very quietly and only doing house guests in the dining room for the first month.

Frequently we would have dinner with them, and it was very informal. Apart from the B&B owners who pulled the curtains down our first guests were thoroughly charming and were an enjoyable baptism into hosting a bed and breakfast guesthouse.

The fact that it was quiet could be partly attributed to the fact that someone from Tasmania's tourism department visited us about a month before we opened and recommended that such a stately property catering to the upper end niche market with just three rooms would not need to join the government run wholesaler, Tasmania's Temptations Holidays. They were incorrect and we were vacuous in not doing more research. Had we have participated prior to opening we would have been in the new brochure for the following year from May 1996 to May 1997. As it happened, we were too late for the previous year and now we were to be left out of the next year. By the time the peak season in January was on us we were saying "where the bloody hell are you?" In those days if you were not in the Temptations book you were not anywhere, because nobody knows you exist. We then realised we had other idiots in this industry to contend with and that we had better sharpen up or we would not be in business very long. Ever the eternal optimists, we decided we needed a mission statement. My sense of humour got the better of me; it went something like this :-

To boldly go where no other guesthouse has gone
To seek out previously unknown life forms as potential guests
To gain knowledge of undiscovered markets
To explore the final frontiers of accommodation
Ormiston House – the next generation!

That was 25 years ago, and I had a more impetuous sense of humour. This of course was not the official mission statement. It did however take pride of place on the office wall. The official mission statement which we used in our business plan was as follows :-

To be the premier guesthouse in Tasmania
To offer a higher standard of presentation than other guesthouses
To offer a higher standard of service than any other guesthouse
To offer a higher standard of accommodation than any other guesthouse
To enhance the west coast of Tasmania and Strahan as one of Australia's premier tourist destinations

These days I would just say "fuck the mission statement!"

But we were as keen as mustard and we would race out when the guests arrived to be the first one to welcome them in. In latter days it was more like you go, no you go, no, you go. In any event one of us would make it to the front door. During the last few years we made this easier by installing security cameras. This had the additional benefit of observing time wasters walking into the gardens hoping for a quick look in the house or even worse peeking into guest bedrooms. Yes, you can imagine my response, and you would be quite correct. But regardless of what disaster was happening in our lives we opened the door with a beaming smile and welcomed our house guests heartily with warmth and hospitality

Chapter Seventeen

'where's your fucking note?'

While these wheels were in motion both guests and industry colleagues would say "I bet you could write a book about life in a B & B". At that stage I never let on that it was my intention to write a book. We all laughed and would often speak about some of the funny incidents and not so funny incidents that crop up every now and then. Then, of course, there are the assortment of people one meets in such an establishment. The scene was set; I just had to write this book.

There was one area of concern that I was struggling to reconcile with and that was the appropriate use of profanity within the text of the book. I was no stranger to the use of swear words and even as a young teenager I, and my friends, found cussing very amusing. I recall we would occasionally go to the WH Smith & Sons news stand at the Eastbourne railway station. With great amusement and a fair amount of trepidation we would look for the Penguin edition of Lady Chatterley's Lover. We would see how many times we could find the word 'fuck' or 'fucking' before the attendant would tell us to "clear off". When I joined the Australian Navy, another recruit I met would say 'fuck' with every second word and I found his conversation rather tedious, but not necessarily offensive, so I avoided him. Then there were our navy instructors who delighted in berating us with a cacophony of abusive language which I am sure was launched with the best intentions. Thereafter I found myself using profane language if I considered the situation warranted it. During my naval career in the 60s and 70s this usually meant controlling language when on leave, with some difficulty, and relaxing when once aboard again. I left the navy in the 'mid 70s' and found language in civvy street to be more contained in the retail industry although when the reps got together language relaxed and of course reps, like sailors, love to tell jokes; of course, when speaking with clients I don't recall any bad language in either direction.

The fire service showed me that, like the navy, language was quite colourful. In the airline industry there was far more contact with the general public and language, together with the correct choice of words, was of primary concern especially when flights were cancelled and discussion with passengers could become quite heated. In such cases better to let the customer swear and then choose to discontinue the conversation due to the abuse being delivered.

During the 80s and early 90s customer interaction was a major part of our riverboat business so once again language was contained, and the use of profanity was restricted to 'below decks' and 'behind the scenes' so to speak.

I do recall one day on our boat we had a group of senior citizens, mostly elderly females, for a morning cruise on the Brisbane River. I was skipper on that day and as we departed, I bid them welcome with a short address and then proceeded to play some background music until I started the commentary. What I did not realise was that one of the crew had been playing Kevin 'Bloody' Wilson on the tape deck while we were cleaning and preparing the boat for the cruise. When I turned the cassette tape on the speaker blared out "Hey, Santa Claus you c**t, where's me fucking bike". I quickly changed the tape and got the appropriate music playing, whilst secretly shitting myself, and looked around at the aged passengers some of whom were playing with their hearing aids while others were sitting there with their mouths open wide wondering if they had actually heard what they thought they had heard. We got away with it, I think.

To get where I was going with this profanity thing; when we finally opened, we decided we had better speak with some of the people in the tourism industry. We had already joined the local tourism association but had not introduced ourselves to the regional group on the north coast of Tasmania based in Ulverstone at that time. We made an appointment and when we arrived, we were shown into the office of the regional tourism manager, a wonderful lady who is also a great friend. She was energetic, still is, and very welcoming and from our perspective the perfect person for the job. The welcome and hand shaking got us off to a very affable start quickly followed by a few sentences containing quite a few 'fucks'. I was a little taken aback as this was my first experience of a business meeting where the word 'fuck' was used so freely. I rarely heard Carolyn swear and at that time I don't think she had ever said 'fuck'. Not to me anyway; although I hear it quite frequently now. Carolyn did her best to pretend that she didn't hear 'fuck' and the rest of the meeting progressed well with just a moderate amount of colourful language. We don't get offended easily and we came out of the meeting laughing and quite amused by the experience. We were soon to learn that the use of profanity was becoming quite common place in Tourism related business meetings; OK with me, as I was happy to join in; for Carolyn it took a bit longer.

A few years ago, Quenton, my brother in-law, was attending a meeting with some people here in Tasmania and among the attendees were a number of Mayors from the surrounding districts. The meeting was being chaired by a female state minister and one of the Mayors arrived late and as he entered the room the chair said, "you're late, where's your fucking note". To which the room erupted in laughter. I rest my case; there are going to be quite a lot of 'fucks' in this book.

Chapter Eighteen

'they were disguised as guests'

Surprisingly, or perhaps not, looking after guests in any hospitality establishment is a time-consuming business, and rewarding......if you do it professionally that is.

I should say at this juncture that the majority of our houseguests have been wonderful people and we have enjoyed their company immensely. Considering that for 21 years we entertained a considerable number of guests per year in our humble establishment, I can say that only a very small percentage have pushed the boundaries to the 'enth' degree. Given that we catered for over 4000 houseguests a year, that would equate to a small number of people; some of which have left an indelible, and somewhat poignant, place in our memories. On occasions other houseguests have shared our views as they too are affected by the occasional example of bad manners exhibited by fellow travellers. They have said to us "How do you tolerate such people?" or "I hope that doesn't happen too often." We, of course, say that these instances are rare; which they are. Well, for the most part anyway. Probably a few guests per year have been downright unpleasant to deal with and I suspect that it was the 'fringe people' that have inflated my recollections of problematic guests. If I were to be brutally honest then I would have to consider that at times I possibly may have contributed to the situation; possible, I suppose, but I doubt it. I suspect that Carolyn may have a different opinion but whose book is this anyway.

For a small establishment such as ours, a small percentage of problematic guests would not be a big deal and certainly nothing to get overly upset about; you would think. However, if one looks at large accommodation establishments that deal with hundreds of thousands of people a year then difficult guests are going to rock up to your doorstep on a daily basis.

Let's face it we have all been in the vicinity of people either whinging or exhibiting bad manners in restaurants and hotels. I, like many of us, would have felt sympathy on many occasions for the hospitality staff trying to deal with difficult situations to their best ability. I would say that working in the hospitality industry would be a breeze compared with some other retail sectors. At least when on holiday the majority of visitors would be in a reasonable frame of mind....................or so we thought!

There are, however, the borderline cases that seem to drift in and out; not causing too much offence but have us shaking our heads…. "Did he really say that?" or "I can't believe they did that". *Persona non gratia*, but how were we to know? …………they were disguised as guests!

If I were to ask anything of the readers it would be to maintain a sense of humour while I bag out some individuals and generalise about other demographics. We do, however, have one cardinal rule in hospitality. That is, we don't personally identify anyone publicly who incurs our ire and out of courtesy we keep the identity of all, including royalty, VIPs and dignitaries who stay with us, confidential. I know that there have been exceptions to this rule where the media gets hold of some juicy information and the situation goes into freefall. In the case of high-profile guests, I for one do not envy their predicament in finding a place where they can relax and take some time off. I will also say that all of the VIPs that have stayed with us have been delightful and courteous people and only one VIP dinner group, who were staying elsewhere thank god, displayed what I would call disgusting manners and appalling behaviour. I have heard other truly appalling tales from some of our peers and perhaps good fodder for a sequel.

In our case not only did we operate a B & B Guesthouse, we also operated a restaurant open to the public. Before we opened, a fellow operator, with a similar premises, not too far away, said in relation to the restaurant, "Don't do it."

We laughed the comment off, thinking he was joking or may have been afraid of losing some business to us. In reflection that was not the first warning we got about opening a restaurant. It was the same operator who warned us to be careful when employing chefs.

The essence of hospitality is respect; mutual respect. Hosts need to respect their guests and customers need to respect the people that are providing the service. In B & Bs it goes double for both parties. The host in a B & B is usually the owner of the premises and is making their home available to the customer. The customer should appreciate and respect that they are a guest in someone's home. The host should welcome the guest in a friendly manner and bestow genuine hospitality. Of course, a fee is charged for lodging, but that fee in a guesthouse usually grants privileges not afforded to guests in other forms of accommodation. The host by nature should be gracious and the customer appreciative. That's enough of theory; let's see how it pans out in real life!

Being an owner and operator of a B&B, or similar accommodation establishment, is vastly different than just simply having a job in hospitality or tourism. When employed in a large establishment one would do a shift and then go home. In such cases, a day of altercations with difficult guests will be part of the shift and then handed to another staff member to handle. This would leave the original staff member to go home and enjoy life until their next shift. More difficult issues can also be handed to a duty manager or supervisor who once again are employed, and who also go home at the end of the day.

In any case the staff member need not carry the emotional baggage of the day home with them. They would however hope that any irritations (troublesome guests) had checked out by the time they do their next shift.

The humble B&B, guesthouse etc. owner, however, will have to work with the issues and the guests on a continuous basis until their departure. This usually means one of two things. Firstly, if the B & B owner is skilled enough then the issues can be resolved and if the problem is attitude on the part of the guest then a good B & B owner should be able to get the guest onside; if they can be bothered! Some belligerent guests are beyond recovery in my opinion, but one does need to, 'make an effort'. Secondly it may be that both the owner and guest leave the issues 'in situ' and unresolved. This means that both guest and owner will have a fucking awful time trying to avoid each other for the duration of the stay. This could result in an early departure by the guest, which can present other problems including the enforcement of late cancellation policies; (leaving without paying is the same as shoplifting, that's our story anyway); *physical confrontation* (a push and shove); *abuse* (fuck off and don't come back); *legal action* (shit, they're suing us) *and sincere regret* (fuck it, we'll have to apologise)

Then there is the other contentious issue – The No Show. For fuck's sake it is not rocket science that if a room is left vacant on a particular night then it is a lost sale. Last night's vacant room cannot be sold a few days later. Selling accommodation is not like selling refrigerators or TVs. We can't put the room back on the shelf and sell it three days later. Once the day has gone, so has the vacant room and any associated income.

So, it should come as no surprise to the terminally stupid that if you don't show up for your room then you will be charged. When you make a booking, whether it is in person, on the phone or by direct online booking, you are in effect entering into a contract to purchase. The accommodation will provide a room and you agree to pay for privilege of using that room. If at some late stage, and in accordance with the cancellation policy, you choose not to stay then stiff shit my friend – you pay.

Some guests will argue the point, threaten legal action or a bad review but an accommodation provider would be an idiot if they did not stand their ground.

I recall 25 years ago that many small accommodation operators would not even ask for a credit card number to secure a booking. They were asking for trouble. No shows in those days were a regular occurrence, so that is when credit card numbers were requested. Some guests would say no, we would suggest they stay somewhere else. Even then some would no show for no reason and so we would charge their credit card. Sometimes we would get an abusive phone call threatening legal action unless we refunded. Some would lie and say they had a car accident, or they took ill. So why no phone call we would ask?

Other providers would complain about the same experience, so we started taking a 50% deposit and others followed. From that time on we rarely had a no show or even an argument if they indeed did not show up for the booking. Except from totally belligerent morons.

I must state categorically that it is essential to have a very clear and concise cancellation policy that is sent to the client as soon as they make the booking. It is also essential to verbally advise them that if a cancellation is made after a certain date then full charges will apply.

It is amazing how normally honest people will descend into blatant untruths and hostile procrastinations in an effort to get out of paying for a room due to the fact that they were total dipshits during their holiday or, as sometimes happened, they totally fucked up their dates and itinerary. In those cases, they expect us to say "that's ok, we'll give you a full refund." Well it's not OK and you're a dickhead. We can't go to our suppliers and say, "we had a lot of no shows this week, so do you mind if we don't pay your account this week." I am sure the bank will understand if we miss a few mortgage payments because we had "a bad week."

Give me strength!

Chapter Nineteen

'a right royal rogering'

What about the owners and hosts of small accommodation establishments? How many small accommodation property owners should do their guests a favour and just sell up, piss off and find something else to do with their lives? Exactly what percentage of owner operators of a B&B, guesthouse, motel or cabin park should genuinely fuck off and find themselves another job?   Equally, would this group be significantly of a higher percentage of the total than that of guests and the other annoying individuals arriving on our doorsteps determined to have a lousy holiday and at the same time giving their hosts and staff the right royal shits? Now, before I give you the impression that I didn't like working in hospitality, and dreaded working with the public, I must emphasise that this would simply not be true. Actually, I did enjoy it. I did enjoy the interaction, and not because I am a born confrontationist.   I do enjoy the company of intelligent people. Did it happen as often as I would like?   Probably, and then again, the annoying individuals didn't arrive in copious quantities but when they did arrive, they tended to take centre stage.

The fact is we have thoroughly enjoyed both the restoration and running the accommodation. The restaurant was a bit of a trial but a great experience for the eight years that we operated it. After those first eight years we decided to concentrate on the accommodation as the early starts and late finishes were getting to us. There were also the restaurant guests; but it is difficult to run a successful restaurant without them.

I suppose I could be jaded by some of my experiences; I could be a tad battle weary with just a touch of shell (guest PTSD) shock; I could have been in the accommodation trenches too long; popping the old head up and getting it shot off. Perhaps I should have been strapped to a stretcher long ago and dragged out under sedation. However, I think it must be our sense of humour that kept us going and those guests that we met that gave us a rich and rewarding experience; and I hope the feeling was mutual.

If fatigue sets in then one can, of course, employ a locum B & B operator to cover for you while you take a 'well earned' break or simply shut down for periods of R & R, the result of battle fatigue. That is if you dare leave your business to someone else, even for a short period of time. We know some couples in the industry that have offered these services and would recommend them without hesitation, but we would be reluctant to hand over our business to someone we did not know. There are a lot of nutters out there, you know.

Closing for a week or two during a quiet period is the best option I think; allow some time for therapy. During your time away stay at a few B & Bs and get your own back like a few of our guests have done to us.

There are many B & Bs out there who just take guests when they feel like it and have a very casual approach to their business. They probably have one or two rooms and they are predominately a lifestyle business. These days Airbnb falls into a similar category. In such cases they operate for a bit of extra cash and one or both have a good retirement income or alternatively one or both still work full or part time. Recently properties have been purchased as an investment and then managed by a business to accommodate short term rentals. i.e. tourism visitors. Each to his or her own but my view is that in today's tourism environment having a casual approach to the way in which a hospitality operation is undertaken, albeit friendly and hospitable, can present with problems. Let's not just blame the guests; owners can be as nutty and badly behaved as some of their guests.

I might add at this time that the tourism and hospitality industry is evolving quickly. The online environment has brought many opportunities but also challenges. In recent years the sharing economy has landed fair and squarely into the lap of the accommodation industry. The playing field is not a level one and other factors such as government policy and council regulations for some and not others are raising many concerns.

Chapter Twenty

'they've been out there breeding'

At the time of writing this little bit, I had just dispatched a couple of house guests, that evening, to a local restaurant. I love that word 'dispatch'. It sounds so final doesn't it? Absolutely charming people. Both couples in the house on that night were from the UK. Was it their reserved politeness that I enjoyed or was it my affinity to the British as it was there that I was born? Was I being drawn back to my roots as a de facto Pom? Was this an awaking of kindred spirits? Maybe, but these were just very nice people and I enjoyed their company; people who are intelligent, articulate, yet down to earth. In fact, we were fortunate in our establishment that we did get a very high percentage of what could be termed 'our sort of people'.

On the other hand, every now and again we got toffee nosed 'would be if they could be' types; total tossers. They waltz in, talking on their mobile phone, waving their hand at me as if to say "I'm talking to James Packer" as they push past and flop into the chesterfield couch talking as loud as they possibly can, so we all benefit from the wisdom dribbling down their chin like some verbal diarrhea.

Yes, we met them with some intermittent frequency. I hate to say it but there really are some dickheads in this world. Could such statements be bad for business? Our business?

Some B & B owners could be trembling at such statements being put into print. Have I possibly alienated some potential guest? I'll take the risk. Not my problem anymore. I will say that if you stayed at our place or most other B & Bs then 99.9% of the other guests will have been fantastic people. Just like your hosts. See, fixed!

Have you ever been standing at a hotel reception and another guest comes down with a query or complaint? Have you wondered what the staff member or B&B owner would like to say?

Questions like....

'How do I turn the tap on?'.......

Answer - Don't you have taps in your house?

Or 'The jug doesn't work'....

Answer - Down here we plug ours in.

or 'The room is full of flies'....

Answer - That's what happens when you remove the fucking flyscreen from the fucking window!

Or 'What time does the nine 'o clock boat leave?'....

Answer - I can't believe you asked me that!

Or 'What room am I in?'

Answer – Reception sir.

I mentioned at the start of this book a comment from a fellow tourism operator on Facebook. That particular post was followed by a few more gems from other industry folk:-

Well, the Victorian lady that once asked me where I was from and was so astounded when I proudly announced my west coast heritage. She replied in astonishment "but you speak English so well" Yes people in Tasmania do speak English. Her three friends were as astounded as I was. **MR.**

You know the set up at the house. If you are sitting in the loo with the door ajar and you think you are alone in the house, then someone walks in OMG! Yes, on call for every enquiry at any time. The WiFi password is so urgent even though all of that info is in the compendium in every room. They are told when they arrive and it's also in large letters on the noticeboard in the guests lounge. **DP.**

Cooking eggs and noodles in the kettle is a thing apparently. Mum had people bring their own electric frying pans and set them up on the bedroom floor and cooking stir fry on the carpet. She could tell by the smell in the room and the splattered food particles matted into the carpet. **DP.**

Or the woman who rang reception and demanded that the river be turned off as it was making too much noise. **MR.**

My dreaded one was when we sat down at the table overlooking the bay for a short break and they would say "how long have you been here?" My reply "two seconds." **LG.**

What time is it going to snow? **TG.**

If I ring my Mum, will she be there? **AD.**

I asked some guests how they slept. "Terrible," they said. "Didn't get a wink of sleep all night due to the noise of that machinery going all night." Turns out the machinery noise was the sound of the waves on the nearby beach. **DP.**

"Will I need a jumper in 6 degrees?" "We don't want it to rain in the rainforest." Bush tucker type person who only eats what he can forage. Wanted us to pick some fresh nuts and berries and could we have them ready for 1.30pm as they had a long drive ahead of them. **MC.**

"How do some of these people travel the world?" **KG.**

Chapter Twenty-One

'wash those dishes, scrub those pots'

My first foray into hospitality, after some thought, was at the age of fourteen when I was asked by a friend to help him carry some bags at a local guesthouse in Eastbourne,

UK. Our job was to take the bags from the bus up to the rooms. We stood by the bus, the bags were claimed by the passengers and we were given a room to take them to. We were going to be paid ten shillings each for the job which wasn't bad for about an hour and a half work; this was 1963. I had taken a few bags up when I bumped into my mate and he said have you got any tips yet and I said no. I asked how much he had received, and he said that one man gave him half a crown. I asked him how he got the tip and he said he just dropped the bags and stood there scratching his balls. So next trip I took the bags up and stood there scratching my balls and the man clipped me around the ear and told me to stop playing with myself. These days, if I'm going to scratch by balls, I look around to see if anyone is watching.

My career in hospitality, although I did not realise it at the time (and following the ball scratching incident), started in 1964. It was school holidays and I heard that a dish washer was required in a large 5-star hotel. I needed some pocket money for the holidays so off I went and got the job. I worked there for about 5 weeks in the summer of '64. After about 2 weeks one of the other dishwashers quit and I asked my old school chum Chris Kent to join me, so we ended up spending our school holidays washing dishes in this large upmarket hotel.

In those days my Dad, who was an electrician with British Railways, earned eleven quid a week fixing lights in railway stations around the south coast of England between Chichester and Hastings, with Eastbourne, where we lived, in between. My first week as a dishwasher, working from 7 in the morning to 10pm at night for 6 nights, brought me eleven quid also. My dad was 42, I was 15. That pissed him off a bit I can tell you.

The hotel was called the Cavendish. It was on the seafront at Eastbourne and busy as hell during the summer. Eastbourne has a wonderful Edwardian façade on the seafront with impressive residential buildings and hotels. The waitering staff were from France and Spain and they took Chris and I under their wings and taught us how to swear in French and Spanish. "Mierda, Que te joden, je ne m'en fous pas, faire chiere, no me importa, vete la mierda". The words don't really need translation. They were great guys. The rest of the back of hotel staff were, how should I say this? A bit sus? Now I am not a snob but as a '15year old' who had a reasonably strict upbringing and in a pretty good circle of friends some of these workers were bloody uncouth to say the least.

There was no staff changing room for us kitchen hands but there was a room above the scullery with no windows. It was also the makeshift bedroom of an old guy who had worked in the hotel since he was a little tacker. Now this old fella was about eighty if he was a day. When I arrived in the morning, he would be asleep in a pile of old soiled

104

bed linen and blankets. Old hotel stock that was supposed to be thrown out was my guess as the old timer looked after the garbage collection in the service areas and kitchen. He must have salvaged some of them for his own use. Initially I was a bit ill at ease going up to this room with this old guy in it, but I soon realised that he was just a lonely old man who wasn't a threat to anyone. So, I would get changed and then get stuck into the silverware which was my first job of the day as well as tackling the breakfast crockery and cutlery as it came in. I had to wash and polish these huge silverware plates, food covers, and god knows what. These days you would be hard pressed to find this kind of stuff, but I used to enjoy cleaning them up and getting them ready for service.

The head or executive chef was a grumpy old bastard who sat on a stool at a davenport desk continually looking over his glasses at all the chefs and kitchen hands. There must have been about 20 chefs in this huge kitchen during busy times. Every now and then he would get up from his desk and walk around and start yelling abuse at the other chefs. He would come over to us and inspect our work, but he didn't seem to have jurisdiction over us as he never roused at us much. That was the domain of a Mr Paterson. One of the cleaners had a big row with him one morning and called him a 'stinking queer'. That was just before he got his marching orders. He came to say goodbye to Chris and myself when he left. Mr Paterson was the catering manager or perhaps the food and beverage manager and a totally unpleasant person. In any case he was our boss and on a daily basis Chris and I had the pleasure of his company.

In 1964 the workplace was a very different environment. I recall that on one occasion I was on the plate scrubber. This was a motor driven contraption consisting of two large wheels with course brushes that almost met in the middle and you would wedge a dinner plate between them and move it around. The trick was to get the plate clean without losing the skin off your fingers. This one day a plate broke as I was moving it around and it sliced into my index finger. Blood came gushing out of a deep cut. One of the waiters got Mr Paterson and he looked at it and said to just put an Elastoplast on it. Now this Mr Paterson must have been all of 25 years of age and now I reflect on it probably just out of catering college and out to make a name for himself. He was a bastard and I have no doubt that he probably made hotel manager somewhere eventually. Anyway, I was in a fair bit of pain and blood was still pouring out of the gash. I also had a concern that a tendon could have been severed. I told one of the waiters that I was heading out to get it stitched up and off I went. I came back about an hour later after five stitches at the local hospital. They put a heavy-duty rubber cover over it like a condom. Paterson just looked at it and grunted and said words to the effect that he didn't think it was that bad. I thought he was going to rouse on me for leaving the kitchen, he didn't, but he did dock my pay for the time I was away.

At the end of our tenure in the kitchen, before we went back to school, we did the right thing and gave a week's notice; Paterson then proceeded to get us to scrub the scullery area from top to bottom. He was determined to get as much out of us as he could in that last week. The waiters went berserk and called him all the names that we understood but I don't think Paterson knew. They told him that Chris and I were the best dishwashers and kitchen hands the hotel had ever had and that he should be rewarding us rather than grinding us into the ground scrubbing his filthy scullery. Anyway, the waiters did a whip around and gave us a bonus before we left. Yep, Paterson was a bastard.

After we went back to school, I was walking down a street close to the seafront and the old fella that lived in the room above the kitchen was sitting on a park bench. I said hello and he told me that he had been kicked out of the hotel. He said that he didn't have anywhere to go. The hotel had not paid him for years and he had worked with the garbage in return for the room and some food. No bathroom or toilet in or near the room for all those years. About a month later someone told me he was found dead on that same park bench. Poor old buggar. Paterson probably kicked him out. Has hospitality changed at all over the years? You may well ask. I guess there are arseholes in every industry. It just seems a little more personal in hospitality.

My family emigrated to Australia in October of 1964. Chris Kent and I still write to each other and exchange Christmas cards as I do with some other school mates from Eastbourne. I went back in 1998 and we all had a few drinks at the Tally-Ho pub at Old Town. It is great having mates that go back so far.

Chapter Twenty-Two

'Darwin's theory of evolution'

Now some of my hospitality mates would ask me, frequently I might add, "Have you told anyone to fuck off lately Mike?" Of course, I haven't, but there have been many occasions in the past 24 years that I have physically felt like saying it. The ones that have tested my patience didn't get the full force of my venom. I prefer to just open the front door and gesture that they leave.

This book is not about lampooning any group, or individual as I will give guests and B & B owners an equally good rogering and some of them, quite frankly deserve it. The trouble is that the oddballs in our industry give bed and breakfast accommodation a bad reputation and at the same time tarnish us all individually with that same brush. Now having said that one would think there must be far more oddball and irritating guests than there are oddball and irritating owners of accommodation properties. And have I already mentioned that they are out there breeding? No; well they are.... and probably in our establishments as well .... perish the thought, we'll let laundry handle it!

The fact is that even though we (property owners) are generally pleasant, well behaved, polite and courteous there are occasions when our metal is tested and, god forbid, we crack. I have cracked a few times in front of guests, although relatively mildly. More often than not, I contain myself, and when in the back of house, out of earshot, let loose with a number of expletives.

I recall a family of three arriving; the booking was in advance for two adults only. They booked our two-bedroom suite; one room has a queen bed and the other a standard double. The booking was made online. I explained that as there were three persons then there would be an extra charge for the third person. The husband objected and said that the suite has two beds and that he has paid for the extra bed. I stated that the price he paid for was for two persons only and that if there were three persons then he should not have made a two-person booking. He again protested and insisted that he would only be paying the standard room cost as quoted for two persons. He clearly indicated that he was prepared to continue arguing. I walked towards the front door, opened it and said, "I'm not here for an argument, go and stay somewhere else" and gestured that they leave. On the way out he said, "Have a nice day." ...... I did.

I was tempted to say, "Fuck off", but I didn't.

It is not unusual for guests to understate the number of guests arriving. Frequently they will not include their children in the booking instead choosing to argue with reception. Some will insist that children were included when the price was quoted. Others will deliberately not mention they have children because the property states children under a certain age are not accommodated. The fact is that it is not uncommon for guests to lie their heads off and try to screw the property for the best possible price. In this situation they will hope that the reception or property owner will not wish to have an open argument and that the property will capitulate to their dishonest requests.

Groups of students, in particular, hide in the vehicle and just 2 will present at reception. If the host or reception is astute, after verification of a room for 2, will offer to get the bags from the vehicle. The students will protest but the host will insist only to find 4 or 5 students hiding under blankets as they open the door. The reception or host will then indicate whether they are prepared to take a booking for the correct number of people. I would prefer to say, "Fuck off." This only happened a few times to us because our entry rack rate of over $200.00 per night turned most of them away when they knocked on our door.

There are people out there who will put it over you any way they can on the premise that accommodation operators are desperate for customers and if they push the issue then they will win and get a bargain. Sometimes it works but not always.

Chapter Twenty-Three

'we may meet again one day'

We did have some interesting cretins in for dinner one night. They were staying at another property where they had dinner the previous night. One was a VIP, an ex-prime minister of another country. He had his wife with him, poor suffering lady, an English minder and an Aussie minder. The English minder wasn't half bad, the Aussie guy was a total 'prat'. The VIP thought he was above everyone else and I am dying to tell you who it was, but I won't. The VIP treated his wife like a second-class citizen which annoyed the hell out of Carolyn.

They ordered fresh crayfish among other things along with 10 other dinner guests that night. Interestingly we also had a film crew who were shooting us for a travel show. Our accommodation was full, so the film crew had to stay at the cabin park. They did however dine with us and film the next day; they were also in the restaurant this particular night.

The Aussie 'prat' decided to get drunk and played around with his crayfish complaining that there was no meat in the head. Now anyone who knows crayfish knows that the organs are in the head not lumps of meat, which is found in the lower half of the body and tail. There are bits up there, but the brown bits get flushed out so that it presents well.

So, the stupid moron was lifting his crayfish up and throwing it down on the plate being a total embarrassment to himself and his table.

While I was talking to other dinner guests the VIP started tapping his glass with his spoon. I just ignored him and looked around as if to say, "what's that noise?"

I was returning to the kitchen with both hands holding plates when the 'prat' comes up behind me and tells me there was no meat in the head of the crayfish. I tell him that there is no meat in the head of the crayfish just organs and if he likes I will cut one in half to show him. He starts getting obnoxious (more) and tells me how much he knows about seafood and that if his party don't get their dessert within 10 minutes, they will be leaving without paying their bill. Now my first thought was to drop the plates and drop him as well, but you can't do that can you? Tempted!

He turns and walks away and if that had happened now, I would have grabbed the prick and marched him out of the house; a publican can do that. God knows I did it plenty of times on my boat with obnoxious drunks.

I went into the kitchen and told Carolyn who said she would fix it. Good, as I was too angry.

She took the dessert order and got them out in double quick time and made a point of serving and speaking with the VIP's wife first, who was obviously embarrassed by the others. This was Carolyn's ploy to annoy the misogynistic males. Then when it came time to pay she said well if your cray was not up to standard I can't charge any of you as all the crays were the same yet for some reason yours was different to which the VIP objected (his only saving grace) and the three paid in full and the 'prat' was not charged for his crayfish. The other three read the prat's horoscope as they were walking across the car park.

I phoned our associates where they were accommodated, and he just laughed. I got the impression he sent them to us to avoid serving them again at his place. He referred to the VIP as a 'villager'.

As a dignitary you would have to watch how you behave because sooner or later you will end up on the internet or in the media somewhere. I have promised myself that if I ever see the 'prat' in question in an airport or wherever I will make myself known. If you are out there and haven't been throttled by a restaurateur yet we may meet again one day under different circumstances.

Chapter Twenty-Four

'a few words of advice'

Advice to guests contemplating arriving early

If your accommodation property tells you that check-in time is 2.30pm, then don't turn up at 11am expecting a room. In fact, don't turn up at 7.30am like two of our idiot guests did one day and, believe it or not, were not only surprised but very put out that their room wasn't available. Your host will allocate a check-in time for a very good reason. More than likely it is because the room will not be ready before that time. Perhaps it is easier to explain if we say that the guests check out at 10am, some may have an extended check out time of 11am. Then the housekeeper, which in most cases is your host in a small establishment, will clean the room, change the bed linen, clean the en-suite, replace towels, clean the windows, vacuum the carpets, dust the furniture and fittings and replace the toilet requisites. By the time your host or housekeeper has done between five and ten rooms it would be no surprise that it usually about 2.30pm. If the cleaning gets done a little earlier and the house is ready then your 'poor something host' has got some minutes or an hour if they are lucky to have some time to themselves and even grab some lunch if they are fortunate before more delightful guests come knocking. So, don't check in early ...in fact stay away for as long as you can. I know you think your host is just dying to meet you but don't kid yourself, they like to get the house ready first.

Advice to hosts about early arrivals

I know you are under pressure and you have still got more rooms to clean and the dog just crapped on the grass next to the clothesline and you stepped in it. I know that the 'buggars' were not supposed to knock on the door until after 2.30pm but hey.... there they are. I know you are still in your cleaning clothes because the housekeeper called in sick due to getting drunk the night before and your stand-by cleaner wasn't available. You still haven't finished cleaning the kitchen and you haven't even started the vacuum cleaner. Yes, I know that you sent them some travelling tips so that they would get the most out of their journey and see all the sights along the way. But hey, guess what. They didn't bother to read them did they and they know that you said check-in is from 2.30pm but they don't give a shit do they?

Brush yourself off, smile and open the door.

'Hello, you're a bit early,' you say with a smile from ear to ear. "Come on in, I'm (insert your name here) and welcome to (whatever your establishment is called). Your room should be ready shortly so come into the lounge and I'll make you a cup of tea." Etc. etc.

What you would really like to say and can't is …..(But you might say it under your breath as you make your way to the door).

"Oh, for fuck's sake what is the matter with you people? I've only just said goodbye to last night's guests. Give me a fucking break."

But we can't say that, can we?

It does amaze us though that some guests turn up to check in when last night's guests are still having breakfast. How do they expect the fucking rooms to be ready when clearly the previous guests are still here? We live in hope that the penny drops when it is their turn to have breakfast and they then realise that their arrival was a bit previous. Whilst most of the guests arrive at a sensible time, and with the knowledge that not only the rooms have to be serviced and the rest of the house as well and on a daily basis, we still get a few that remarkably make the same cloned statement. "We know we are early, but we thought we would stop by anyway."

Why? What did you expect to hear apart from the bleeding obvious? There is a 'check in' time so your room, and the house, will be ready. Good quality guesthouses and B & Bs get cleaned from top to bottom on a daily basis and this takes a few hours.

B & B owners, I find, are usually wonderful people who come from every walk of life and intend, just for a few years, to run a B & B. If, as a few do, they fall into the category of rude hosts then "get another job" would be the advice. Then there is another class of B & B owners who fall into the "weird" category; we have had a few of them stay with us. There are some delightful B & B owners and like us not only do a wonderful job in providing a memorable and accommodating experience but are well travelled and naturally hospitable people. On the flip side we have met a few rotters who were as bad as some of the other guests we have had.

We had one couple some years ago who were total posers. They had the cheek to write to Tourism Tasmania with a list of things we were doing wrong and had the temerity to say that we did not have a door on our en-suite in our premier room. When we received the copy from Tourism Tasmania I just had to go in the room and check. Did we miss something in the restoration? Did I leave a door off after painstakingly creating the doorway tailor made for an original four panel door from elsewhere in the house? What a sigh of relief. After operating Ormiston House for five years I was so fucking relieved to find a door on the en-suite. Now that said a lot for the credibility of the guest.

Do you want to own and operate a B & B? Great...then answer some quick questions.

Do you enjoy the company of people and present with a happy personality, warm and welcoming, affable and friendly? Good start, however, check with your friends first. *You may not be as affable as you think you are.*

Do you prefer to talk about yourself and readily give your opinion on all subjects oblivious to the opinions of others? *Maybe you are not as suited as you first thought.*

Do you have a short temper; lose your cool; demonstrate a tendency to be blunt and curt in conversation? In short would you prefer to say "fuck off" instead of "hello, how are you? *If so, a different career path may be your best option.* Mind you, as I have previously noted, on occasions I have felt like telling a few guests to fuck off, but I never have.

The fact is that you will not infrequently have people present as guests who will give you the shits from the moment you open the door to greet them. They will be anything from serial complainers who should have stayed at home to boring snobs who have a look on their face that gives the impression that they recently stepped in something unpleasant.

There will be grounds I am sure to march some of these people straight back out of the door through which they came and be quite justified in doing so. In the same way that guests will walk out if they do not like the establishment or the behaviour of the host. The fact is it does work both ways, but a guest will be particularly unpleasant in the way in which they express themselves; however, as hospitality owners we need to be tactful in the way that we tell them to fuck off.

e.g. "I am so sorry sir that the house is not to your satisfaction, I do apologise and of course we will refund your deposit."

Better to get rid of the whinging bastard politely than suffer a hostile interchange followed up by a less than complimentary review on the internet or a letter to the editor of a national newspaper. Small businesses can have difficulty in weathering some public criticism, especially hospitality, so avoid it if you can.

One of the issues today is that a complaint can go viral on the internet and inflict a lot of damage. Most review sites allow an owner response but the latitude for an owner is far less than that given to a customer or guest by the site administrator. The trouble with reviewer websites is that they offer the whingers and self-righteous their five minutes of fame on a world stage and many of them have a much higher opinion of their reviews than either you or I would afford them. However, it is now a fact of life with the internet so be careful.

So, if you are considering buying a B & B, guesthouse, boutique or private hotel are you still interested? If any aspect I have mentioned so far puts you off then you can also head a little further downmarket in terms of selling price, standard or star rating where the guests may not be so discerning. That however also brings with the situation other issues such as absconders, trashers, dishonesty, and probably a measure more bad language and even threats of violence. But you can get away with a more confrontational approach to some of the problems. My experience is that the better class of establishment you operate the better class of arseholes you meet.

I must stop here and say categorically that most of the individuals you will meet will be charming and polite and no doubt very nice people. But one prick can ruin your entire day if you let them

Advice to the Complaining Guest

Don't think for one moment that your host is interested in any complaints you have about your journey to this idyllic location. The first thing you're going to say is "My god, what a drive, that road here was appalling." or "This bloody weather, we came here for a holiday not a two week bath" and of course that famous one liner" What's the weather forecast for tomorrow, hope it's better than today?"

Instead why don't you greet your hosts with the same smile that you expect from them? Why present yourself as a whinging half-wit from the moment that the door opens. I am sure your host will come to that conclusion within a short while anyway. If you are such a pessimist or serial complainer, why go on holidays and bore the shit out of us with your unpleasant company. Stay at home and give your neighbours the shits or was it them that gave you the money to go on holidays in the first place.

Be a happy and pleasant camper right from the word go or piss off. Why go on holidays and be miserable when you can stay at home and do that. Make the most of your holiday and experiences. Accept the fact that things do go wrong from time to time but if you maintain a light-hearted attitude and a positive outlook and above all remain a friendly person you will get the most from your fellow travellers and from your hosts.

And face the facts; the roads are no worse than in your own state or county. The weather is the same wherever you go. Sometimes it rains and sometimes it does not. If you want sunshine every day go to an area that has sunshine every day. If you want a warm climate go to Queensland and if you want lush green wilderness, and a refreshing shower or two go to Tasmania. It's not rocket science so stop whinging about the weather. You are boring us shitless with your pathetic ramblings.

Advice for the Complaining Host

Lead by example and don't you complain about what a shit day you are having. They don't want to hear that. Greet them with a smile and keep your troubles and medical complaints to yourself.

Try and get to the front door before your guests do. Put a sensor in the driveway so you know they are arriving. Open the door before they get there and greet them with a smile. You probably were hoping that they were coming later but hey, that's life and you did say check in from 2.30pm didn't you? If you wanted them to arrive later then you should have said so in your confirmation letter or email. What was that? You don't send them a confirmation letter or email. You don't give them an arrival time. You don't suggest all the interesting places they could visit along the way. 'You dickhead.' What the hell are you doing in this business? You are just as big a tosser as some of your house guests. Wake up to yourself and give them a big smile, do a brief and friendly check in and welcome them with a bit of afternoon tea. That will keep the buggars happy for a little while before they start pestering you for the information you should have sent them when they made their booking. What's that? you didn't send them any information...dickhead!

I feel much better now.

Chapter Twenty-Five

'you're the bloody spoon salesman'

One evening we had a group from one of the mines. They had a Malaysian Prince with them who ran a smelting operation in Asia. So, we set a table of 10 on one table in a closed off area and houseguests in the other dining room. So, the buggars all decided to come in together. We get the orders in and I kept them entertained with drinks and tried to slow the process down a little in the bar and get them into the dining room in an orderly fashion. I organised the houseguest's orders in the bar and the group in the closed off section a few minutes later.

The idea was for the houseguests to get seated and entrees out first before we tackled the group. All was going well with entrees out for the houseguests and apart from a corked wine, a '94 St George Coonawarra from memory, I had the mining group under control. Entrees cleared in both rooms and then time for mains to come out. The waitress had her mind somewhere else so when instructed to take the first two mains to houseguests she decided to take them to the mining group instead. So, when she went to the wrong dining room the head of the group said, "ah beef!" and directed that to be sent to the Malaysian prince and the other plate to another person at the table.

When the waitress returned to the kitchen, she was given another two plates for the houseguests and instead looked at the table layout on the wall with a frown as she went out and then stopped. "What have you done?" enquired Carolyn, whose sixth sense just went into overdrive. Then came the confession.

"Shit", said the chef, "fuck, fuck, fuck, fuck"

"Buggar," said Carolyn.

The chef started pounding his forehead on the stainless-steel kitchen bench.

I came into the kitchen. "Were those meals meant for the mining group?"

Carolyn took charge immediately and told the chef to re-allocate the next meals; the chef promptly threw the appropriate contents on the stove; I circulated and kept the peace in the dining rooms with a new wave of drinks; whispered in the ear of the mining group that, sorry, a short delay. The prince apparently was used to eating first so he was happy to start. Within 15 minutes all at the table had their meals....by taking two at a time the delay did not seem that bad and as the plates hit the table they just started.

I sent the last houseguests in the queue up to our history room for a walk which they thought was a great idea and they took their drinks with them.

I guess you had to have been there.

Another evening the same waitress was on and we had four people from the UK in for dinner that were staying in another accommodation property. I had seated the group and remarked to the kitchen that there was a chap that looked just like the spoon salesman from Fawlty Towers (Bernard Cribbins) in the group. The waitress had taken food orders and even though not her job, was given a wine order at the same time but she negated to tell me.

After their food order was taken, I passed by a few minutes later and this spoon salesman said...

"Excuse me, excuse me, we haven't had our wine yet," in a thick Yorkshire accent.

"I'm sorry I said, I had no idea you had ordered wine."

"Well we gave it to the girl, didn't we?"

I apologised, hurried off and got the wine order, back to the table, poured, apologised again and just as I made my exit the spoon salesman said, in that same thick Yorkshire accent.

"It's a bit like Fawlty Towers here."

I could have throttled the little prick.

I suppose I could have said, "you're right and you're the bloody spoon salesman", but I didn't.

Chapter Twenty-Six

'more advice'

Advice to the Know it all Guest

So, you know everything, do you? You are the quintessential smartarse. How do we recognise you? I'm sorry to say but you are so bloody obvious it "beggar's belief." You have a bit of a swagger as you get out of the car. You leave your wife to extract herself from the car by herself as you stride towards the entrance determined to assert your importance from the first instance. You probably don't realise it, but you made a complete ass of yourself with your previous host and when your back was turned the other guests commented on the fact and they hoped you weren't staying long. They were also hoping that you wouldn't talk to them over drinks as no one likes a smartarse. Be careful as many small accommodation operators communicate on a regular basis so if you were a prick last night and behaved badly the word is probably out there already.

You are greeted by your host but before they have an opportunity to finish their greeting you butt in and continually try to pre-empt the conversation making it perfectly clear that whatever you have to say is far more important than the information your host is trying to impart.

You are usually the one who heads off in the wrong direction because you didn't listen to the directions you were given. You have probably parked your car in the wrong place and rudely interrupted your host when they were just about to offer you a complimentary drink at the bar before dinner. You arrive at the bar as everyone else is partaking of their free drink and chatting together because you didn't bother to listen to your host tell you what time complimentary drinks were. You will probably be either too early for breakfast or too late. You will wonder why you missed the scenic cruise or couldn't find the car park or in fact missed out on the courtesy vehicle. Why? Because what you have to say is far more important than what everyone else has to say. We know that smartarses sometimes travel in pairs and the female companion can be just as bad if not worse; especially if they are the type that likes to jangle copious quantities of gold and jewellery while continually tossing their stole over their shoulder. Everything is frightfully this or frightfully that and she has the habit of walking away as the host, or staff, are speaking with them. Little do they know that while this is going on other more reasonable guests give the host or staff member a wry smile or shake their head. Some even approach and say, "what an obnoxious person...we think you are doing a sterling job". When I am out and about, I enjoy going up to obnoxious people who give hospitality staff a hard time and tell them what I think of them. Hey, it's payback time!

Advice to the Know it all B & B Host

Now this applies just as much to smartarse hosts as well and believe me, they have been out there breeding as well. What are you trying to prove by 'out-talking' your guests? Is it an inferiority complex that makes you do this, you goose? You accomplish absolutely nothing by waffling on. No-one is really that interested in you trying to convince your guests that you know more than they do....and in fact what do you know? You probably should know that you are in the wrong job and guess what; your guests know that as well. There is nothing worse than when your guests roll up eager to meet their new hosts only to find that the bastard is a total know it all who must be 400 years old. How else could he or she be so qualified in every bloody subject on earth from the bowel habits of great sloths of the Amazon jungle (being a slow mover has its disadvantages) to the total mass of all the planets in our solar system? $(2,666.6996 \times 10^{24}$ kg) approximately according to NASA if anyone was curious. Best you bite your tongue and treat your guests with the same respect that you would expect from them. Don't be a smartarse!

Chapter Twenty-Seven

'a collection of stories'

Croissants, Germans and Sea Dogs

I laugh about the German lady who was sitting in our breakfast room. This was during our first year from memory when we only had three rooms. She was alone and said her husband would be along shortly. I asked her if she would like some 'hot croissants.' She looked at me with a quizzed look on her face and said, "Do you have Pavarotti?"

It was my turn to have a funny look on my face. "I'm sorry?"

"Placido Domingo?" she asked

God knows what the expression on my face looked like.

"Well do you have Dame Joan Sutherland?"

"I'm sorry," I said, "don't you like the background music."

She replied, "the music is fine, you just asked me if I would like some opera songs."

When I returned a few minutes later I pointed to the croissants and said, "this one is Pavarotti and this one is Placido Domingo."

During the time that we operated the restaurant at Ormiston House for eight years there were some funny moments. One evening we had a full house and, as usual, most of the tables occupied. As was customary we played some quiet background music and I enjoyed finding music that would suit the guests and the ambience.

This particular evening, we had fairly elderly diners, and quite a few English. I love the English and their sense of humour and their obvious reserve. I had chosen a selection of World War II songs.....White Cliffs of Dover etc. you get the drift.

The first table on the left by one of the windows was an elderly English lady sitting by herself. The music was not particularly loud, but this lady was humming away to herself and obviously enjoying it.

We had some diners joining us from another accommodation establishment and a table of four were Germans. It occurred to me after they joined us that some of the music on the CD was not exactly complimentary to Germans. I realised this just as Flanagan and Allan were giving Hitler a serve. Shit! I raced to the CD and changed the music.

As I was passing the elderly lady to my left she said, "You changed the music, I was enjoying that."

"I'm so sorry," I whispered in case any other table could hear me, "we have just had some Germans join us, so I changed the music."

"Germans," she said not exactly quietly, "who won the bloody war anyway?"

One evening I was chatting to a house guest in the bar and he asked if I had been in the navy. Probably because of the maritime memorabilia on the walls I would think. I said "yes" and he said, "me too and I am still in actually."

At that time, I noticed a couple of ladies needing drinks in the restaurant, so I excused myself and went to their table. While I was taking their drink order they said they noticed me having a chat to the gentleman in the bar. I said yes, I used to be in the navy, and turns out that he is in the navy right now. The chap is probably an admiral, I said jokingly. When I went back to the bar I said, "and what do you do in the navy", expecting him to say warrant officer or something like that. He said, "actually I've just been made rear admiral." Smiling I said, "I paid off a petty officer. Twenty-five years ago we would hardly be sharing a drink across the bar, let alone in my own stately home."

We both smiled and chatted for another half hour or so. What a nice chap he was and so unlike many of the officers that I remember.

The benefits of being a good guest.

Peter from Michigan arrived. Peter stayed with us 14 years ago and remembered the great hospitality that we showed him as a solo traveller. This visit he brought his partner and another female friend and specifically wanted to show them our house and introduce Caro and I to his partner and friend.

His best memory of his Tasmania holiday was that I took the trouble to drive him to Ocean Beach in my 4wd and show him some of the natural wonders and wildlife on the west coast near Strahan. This was not an organised trip and is not something that happens with every guest. In Peter's case he was travelling by himself and he is just the nicest person. There was a huge amount of mutual respect between Caro, myself and Peter. Right from the moment he approached our front door there was an instant camaraderie. Now this happens regularly in this industry and we are no exceptions where the host enhances the visitor experience. We reciprocate, not for financial return but, for the pleasure of showing and demonstrating sincere hospitality. This sincerity is a world apart from the nuances and platitudes that a traveller would experience in their travels usually with larger organisations where staff extend courtesy as a matter of company policy rather than a genuine wish to please the guest. With B & Bs many of the services rendered at no charge by the hosts, as an integral part of the visit, would be charged for by a large hotel. Those extra services by a B & B host would be such things as a local telephone call, a cup of coffee, some afternoon tea, a lift to a nearby tourism attraction or a pick-up during a sudden shower of rain.

In most cases the differences between accommodation can be a simple case of good honest hospitality and friendliness which in so many cases cannot be put into writing, yet so very, very important.

It was interesting that while Peter from Michigan was getting ready to leave another of our house guests, Terry and Veronica from UK, were waiting for me. Terry has an avid interest in 'lighthouses' and we were talking the previous night over a glass or red wine about the lighthouses at Hell's Gates, the entrance to Macquarie Harbour. Terry and Veronica were only staying for 1 night and were heading off to Cradle Mountain the next day. He inquired about driving to the heads and I asked what car he was driving as the gravel road had been roughed up recently with log trucks and other traffic. I suggested that the next morning before he leaves that I take them for a drive so they could get some photographs and I would give them a commentary along the way. When we returned, about an hour later he said, "now how much do I owe you?" I replied, of course, no charge. It was good for me to get out of the house anyway and I enjoy good company. I also enjoy showing visitors some of our 'out of the way' places and the stories about why places are named.

Just as Peter remembered our drive to Ocean Beach so many years ago so too will Terry and Veronica remember their drive to Hell's Gates. I doubted if Caro and I will be here at Ormiston House 14 years later, but the visitors may return one day and meantime they will tell their friends about the hospitality they received on their travels.

Now I, or other hosts, can't take everyone out for a drive or spend a specific hour or two with just one person but when the situation presents itself and we meet likeable people is sits very naturally in the whole scheme of things to extend the hand of genuine hospitality.

It is interesting how the mood of a house can change dramatically. It only takes one tosser and that harmony can be shattered like a pane of glass in a storm. Two days after Peter and Terry departed, I had been doing some extensive pruning on some trees and the sensor on the front gate sounded. Carolyn was probably in the laundry and so I wandered out in my gardening clothes, just in case there was a guest checking in. I met a guest in the foyer who had obviously checked in earlier however there was a distinctly unpleasantness about this person. Made more obvious by my previous harmonious interaction with recently departed guests. Emphasis on departed and not deceased!

I exchanged some cordiality only to receive a gruff response and almost aggressive persona. Now I am a modest 5ft 6", this guy was a bit shorter than me. Now whether this gentleman had 'little man syndrome' or had 'shit on his liver' for some reason I was not to know at the time, so I smiled and busied myself checking the window for guests. He suggested that if I was checking for guests that one had just departed, and I should consider getting closed circuit TV. I mentioned we had considered it but moving around the house was part of what we do, and in any case, we enjoyed interacting with guests. We parlayed for another minute or two but try as I may to get a smile or bring some positives into the conversation was met with almost smart arsed, know it all comments. He mentioned he worked on an oil rig and they had cameras everywhere. I thought straightaway that we have a man who works in a dangerous often hostile environment where social skills are probably not a pre-requisite for handling drilling equipment and his job could be extremely stressful at times. However, one of the nicest chaps I have met recently was also in the same industry, so my brief psycho analysis was not presenting me with a stereotype.

Later that evening, around 9pm, this particular chap rang our little bell outside our office. I said to Caro, who was cooking our dinner, that I would go and see who wanted us. I opened the kitchen door and he was standing at the office a short distance away. He looked at me and said, "A glass of red wine," once again in an abrupt and most unfriendly manner. No please or other cordiality. He was also complaining that the cups from the room had not been returned after they left them out to be washed. I said I would check it out and get some clean cups for him. (why they couldn't wash their own cups is beyond me). I followed him to the bar and there was another couple there whom I had not met previously so I introduced myself to them. I asked them if they would like a drink also, the lady declined, the gentleman asked for a cold beer which I immediately served. I turned my attention to the original gentleman, poured him a liberal glass of a nice shiraz for which he paid cash. We only charge pub prices for our wines and they are better quality than the pub anyway so no chance of a complaint about price or quality. There was no 'thank you' unlike the other house guests seated who were most polite and appreciative.

When I returned to the kitchen I remarked to Carolyn about the rude little prick and of my earlier conversation. She had already told him that the bar was open for guests before they go out for dinner and would be closing at 8.30pm. I served him and the others at 9pm after they returned from dinner in town. I don't mind doing this later in the evening provided it doesn't turn out to be a late session. We try and have dinner ourselves at a time when the guests are out of the house having their own dinner and less likelihood of us having our own dinner interrupted although it does happen frequently. As much as we would like, we can't put a sign up saying "Piss Off, we are having our dinner!"

Anyway, back to the little prick. Caro said that he was the same with her, gruff, bordering on unpleasant and rude. She said he was having some disagreement with his wife (this happens quite a bit, funny eh!) and this could well be the reason for his manner. She told me that the three ladies, he and his wife were travelling with two other ladies, were probably just as peeved with him as we were as they and his wife were back in their rooms and he was alone in the bar. I deduced that he was giving them the shits as well as us.

Now this is where Caro's attributes and skills kick in. "Don't worry," she said, "I'll work on him and get him round." Meaning that she would embark on an attitude changing strategy between then and breakfast the next morning.

"Well good," I said, "You can serve the prick because obviously his wife and travelling companions have had enough of him as well. I thought the bar was supposed to be closed by this time."

Caro plated up and quickly dashed out to the bar and he was sitting there by himself whereby she poured him another liberal glass of red wine which would last him until we finished dinner.

We finished dinner by which time he had gone to his room and so we closed the bar and finished for the night. The next morning after the guests had finished breakfast, I asked Caro how the 'Little Prick' had gone. Apparently, he was his usual gruff self when he came out and complained that the computer in the business centre was not working. This type of comment is usually linked to the fact that they have not turned it on. He stated that he needed to use the computer to print out travelling directions to their hotel in Hobart. Caro asked where they were staying and that she would print out directions and a map for them. He then made some negative comment for which his wife interjected (good for her) and told him that Carolyn knows what she is doing. When Caro returned with coffee, croissants and a map with directions he had no choice but to say thank you and for the remainder of breakfast and departure was polite and thankful. What a turnaround...she's good at that! Me? Sorry I won't bring the morons around. If they arrive averagely happy then I will do whatever I can to make their stay as memorable as I can but if they show me discourtesy or bad manners then either Carolyn takes over or if she is away for any reason they will have to come around by themselves. Whilst I have got close to throwing a guest out for bad behaviour it has never got to that stage. I have suggested a couple of times at 'check-in' that they stay somewhere else and they have accepted my recommendation.

No wonder the army didn't want him

We brought a new room on-line in early 2000. In fact, the last few days prior to NYE 1999 were hectic and I didn't sleep for two days finishing off tiling and painting as we had guests on the 31st December. Consequently, I did leave off a few tiles behind the cast iron pedestal of the wash basin, which incidentally was an original re-enamelled 1870's model. However, you would need to get on your hand and knees and push your face behind the pedestal to see the missing tiles.

As usual we were extremely busy for the first few months of the year. Other jobs and priorities (like looking after house guests) took precedence and so I forgot about the missing tiles. That was until we greeted a new guest, a recently retired high-ranking army officer. Caro was away at the time (why is she usually away when we get the difficult ones).

I showed them to the room and did the usual meet and greet, very warm and friendly. He made the comment that the army had decided that they didn't need him anymore. (It became apparent to me very quickly why this was so).
Within 10 minutes his wife caught up with me and said that they didn't think the room was five-star. (the old RACT scheme was in effect at that time, and as we had remote control central heating and climate control we slipped into the 'five-star category'.)
I apologised (don't be so surprised). And I took her to see our premier room which she agreed was definitely five-star. I then offered her and her husband the room at no extra charge for their two day stay. She however declined and said that they would stay where they were as they had unpacked their suitcases.
We heard no more from them during their entire stay. They did not talk to us; I even recall that they did not come in for breakfast which was included in the tariff. They did not dine in house and they did not say good-bye when they departed.

Two weeks later we get a letter from Tourism Tasmania asking us for an explanation into a complaint and included was a copy of the letter from the retired army officer. The letter also included photographs of weeds in my garden, two flags that were frayed at the ends and the missing tiles behind the wash basin. There were about 2 pages of problems, none of which the guest raised with us, no mention that we had offered them the premier suite shortly after arrival.

My reply was polite and apologetic but I did suggest that the retired officer get used to the fact that he is now out of the army and that in small business there is not a platoon of lower ranks dedicated to weeding the garden, mending flags and painting rocks. I added that the preceding three weeks of continual rainfall and high winds had contributed to the condition of the garden and flags and that such work was carried out by myself when the weather improved. Etc, etc

Having served in the military I knew exactly where he was coming from. The housing and grounds surrounding serving high ranking officers are kept immaculate by a plethora of individuals as a priority within establishments. There would not be a blade of grass out of place and every stone on the driveway would be dressed by the right. But there is a real world out there and the transition to that real world can be traumatic for some. Going from that world where everyone salutes you to a real world where you are just the same as the man next to you would be a bit of a shock for some I would think. In the same way that a steward in the services, who provides similar services as the host in a B & B, is a low ranking enlisted person in contrast to the host of a B & B who can also be a retired professional from any of a number of doctrines and does not deserve to be looked down upon by people who have allusions of grandeur. So General, get fucked!

Not a happy camper

One day, 1999 from memory, we had a Long Table tourism function in Strahan. The Premier of Tasmania, the late Jim Bacon, was the guest of honour. I was Chairman of West Coast Tourism at the time and was required to look after the Premier and make a speech or two.

Because this was such a big occasion a few of the restaurants were closed, ours was one of those, and we had to leave our guests at 7.30pm to attend. Our chef was also assisting the long table venue. In retrospect we should have totally closed ourselves and not taken any guests. It was just our luck that one of the guests was not happy. We had no trouble at all with the other three couples in house and they wished us well and said, "off you go and have a good evening." This one guest complained from the moment we told him that there was only one restaurant and two hotels open for dinner that night due to a function. He was jumping up and down because there was not enough choice for dinner, that we were going out of the house and that our bar was closing that evening at 7.30pm. He said he was going to complain to Tourism Tasmania; most of the executives of Tourism Tasmania were at the dinner. He was going to write to the head of the local tourism organisation; oh dear, that was me. He was leaving town and was heading to the next town for accommodation and a meal; oh dear, most of the tourism operators from the next town were in Strahan as well and by the time he got there it would be after meal times at the three pubs within driving distance. No-one ever got a letter but if he had been reasonable like the other guests, he would have had a great night with them. It is difficult for some people to realise that even B & B owners are entitled to a life and while we are available most days and most nights 24/7 there are some instances when we either need or are required to be somewhere else. On many occasions, owners will go separately to events so that guests are not left unattended but hey, be realistic. Guests pay for rooms and services not perpetual servitude.

Chapter Twenty-Eight

'things that go bump in the night'

The lady in the grey dress

I recall that during the first year we operated as a guesthouse that I was on breakfast duties and as it often happened, we would hear doors opening and closing. We would leave the kitchen door open a tad to keep an ear out, so to speak.

Most of the opening and closing would be houseguests entering and leaving their rooms. Occasionally, on a windy day, a breeze through an open door or window would cause doors to slam shut.

On this particular morning I had left the houseguests in the breakfast room; 3 couples all chatting nicely over coffee, tea and toast. I was taking the croissants out of the oven and placing them on plates when I heard a door open and close. That's funny I thought. I grabbed the plates and opened the kitchen door and as I turned left, I saw the back of a woman in a long grey dress just turning the corner in the passageway. The dress was trailing on the carpet. I hurried down the passageway hanging onto the croissants and when I got to the corner there was no-one there.

I entered the breakfast room and asked the guests if any of them had left the room. Apparently, they had all stayed in the breakfast room chatting. So, who was it that I had seen?

This happened a few days later, almost exactly the same time but once again she had disappeared, and the guests had never moved from their tables. Since then the sound of doors opening and closing was a common event but no other sightings to my knowledge.

However, it may be that house guests see the lady from time to time but think she is a guest or a staff member.

One afternoon we had a lady arrive with her mother. She was in a foul mood and nothing was right, in fact everything was going wrong. We were under the impression that the booking was for her and her husband. As it happened there were some family issues and she arrived with her mother. We then had to organise another bed for the room and a bit of drama to start with. She was with us for two nights and try as I may there was no pleasing her on that first evening. She dined in house that evening with her mother who I might add was quite OK. The next morning at breakfast she pulled me aside and apologised for her behaviour when she arrived. She told me that she had a massive argument with her husband and hence travelling with her mother instead of cancelling the whole holiday. Then she said something which fairly knocked me off my feet. She said that the nice lady in the Victorian dress had come into her room last night and gave her a hug and told her everything was going to be alright. From then she was as pleasant as can be and when she departed, she was in the best of spirits, pardon the pun.

One of the media staff from Tourism Tasmania were staying with us and over breakfast she thanked us for the accommodation and asked if we had heard from the journalist that had stayed with us a few weeks prior. As it happened, we had not, and she told us that the journalist was rapt over her stay especially the visit she had to her room in the morning. The journalist had retired to her room as guests do and locked her door. At around six in the morning the door opened and a lady in a Victorian dress came in and gave her a cup of tea which she placed on the bedside table. The journalist thought two things. Firstly, I thought I locked the bedroom door and the key is still in the door and secondly what a lovely thing to do for the guests, having an early morning cuppa brought in by a staff member in period costume. She then drifted off back to sleep only to awake with the alarm clock ringing but no cup of tea on the bedside table. Strange she thought. The journalist left early on a cruise but relayed the story to the tourism staff member.

There have been a few guests comment on feeling a presence in the house. Some have said they have seen a small girl standing at the foot of their bed but none of them felt alarmed. I was showing some travel agents around the house recently. Two of them were staying in the house and others were scattered around the town. I took them up to our history room and showed them some old photographs.

When I showed them the photo of one of the Henry wives one of the agents said, "I saw her last night in my room."

Of all the reports we have received I am sure there are more who say nothing but not one guest has shown any discomfort in fact quite the reverse. They seem to be quite privileged that the presence in the house has contacted them in some way.

As I have mentioned previously Ormiston House has an aura of peace and calm and any presence is benign and obviously here to keep an eye on the place.

I asked a couple of tourism operators who operate heritage accommodation if they had any stories to tell. As you can imagine some of them are reluctant to talk in case it is detrimental to their occupancy. However not all people have these experiences and those that do not often lampoon those that believe and feel that they have had an unexplained experience.

One sent me back a quick note as follows just before going to print:-

Yes, great to hear from you Mike, and the production of your book. Two things come to mind. A policeman staying with us had an episode with something sitting on top of him in bed and was unable to get out. The second one relates to a family who asked who was cooking their breakfast when they had booked a self-contained unit. They were adamant someone should be doing it. Hope your book is a success, hopefully we will catch up soon. **WL**

The other email was a bit more detailed:-

It was quite some time ago. A fellow had a strange experience one night. He woke up and said he was paralysed; couldn't speak or move but instead of being himself he was an old woman. Needless to say, he was quite disturbed by the incident once he was himself again. Mum thought it may have been her mother (my grandmother) who had since passed away but whilst alive often slept in that room and had a stroke in bed one night where she was unable to move. She came good for a while and lived for a few years after that although ever since then mum has always made sure there were flowers for Ma in that room. I carried on the tradition mainly because mum kept reminding me. Then 3 days ago in a different room at breakfast a guest said in a semi joking way that he didn't appreciate that a lady come into his room in the night. We were like WTF! Another guest must have wondered into the wrong room. Then he said she was sitting in the chair in the corner of the room; just sitting. He thought at first it was his wife and said Margaret are you OK? There was no answer. Margaret what are you doing there? Margaret was still lying beside him and answered. "Nothing, I was asleep." He said the lady was wearing a type of early 1900s outfit. I told dad and he said, "I'll be buggared." He said a friend that visited them years ago, who claimed to be a psychic, said there were a number of spirits in the house but all good ones that were content and happy. I've never had a spooky feeling here myself. Lately, I stopped with the fresh flowers in the rooms due to slim pickings in the garden. After the incident 3 days ago, John said I think you better start doing the flowers again. We had a French guy stay with us and he must have been traumatised and afraid to leave

the room because he peed in the wardrobe onto the spare pillows.
DP.

Some other experiences

It is not unusual for older properties to have reputations of having ghosts and things that go bump in the night. Carolyn is not a believer and if she experienced an incident, she would self-explain it away I am sure with some reasonable alternative. However, speaking with other accommodation operators, as we have done for many years now, we are not alone in having a presence in the house. Without naming the properties specifically as it is not always their choice to publicise these phenomena.

One Georgian property on the east coast of Tasmania has a night visitor that would walk up the stairs at a certain time most nights and stop outside one specific room. It would them remain there with the occasional creak of a floorboard while it was standing there and then return down the stairs and disappear.

Another property near Launceston had a guest room in what used to be the attic. Items on the dressing table would often get moved or in fact disappear only to be found in another part of the house at a later time.

There were some cottages in the south east of Tasmania where guests would be woken up by someone tapping them on the shoulder.

We had a houseguest who had a five-year old boy with them. I was speaking with the mother in the breakfast room one morning and she asked if we have any ghosts. I told her of my experiences, and she said well you won't laugh at me when I tell you mine. Apparently, they were at Port Arthur a few days prior to staying with us and during the day they were walking around the grounds and the young boy asked his mother who the people were that were following them. She turned around and could not see anyone. The young boy insisted that they were there and one of them was laughing and hiding behind the trees and poking funny faces at him. This continued while they walked around the church ruins as the boy was talking to them.

I then told her about our experience at Port Arthur. While on holiday we did the ghost night tour which for the most part was uneventful until we visited the medical officers house. Underneath was a room with a mortuary slab used for dealing with convict corpses. I say dealing because there was a mention of vivisection. We all stood around the table and the guide said that strange things often happened in the room. While she was speaking, I felt a breeze blowing on my right cheek, like someone was blowing onto it. Then the hood on the person next to me was suddenly pulled down. The guy next to her was just holding his camera when it suddenly started to rewind. Remember these were the days before digital cameras and smartphones. I asked the tour guide where the breeze was coming from and she said nowhere. This is a sealed room. The next day we did a walk around Port Arthur and at one point we were inside the guard tower and I was taking a video. Suddenly the hair went up on the back of my neck and I suggested we leave as I said I felt very uncomfortable.

When we got back to our friend's house, we replayed the VHS video when our friend said stop, and he rewound the video and stopped it right where there was this hideous face on the wall. The pattern of the face was caused by the effects of the peeling plaster and I suppose some shadow. It looked so evil. We also noticed a green mist on the floor which we did not see while the video was playing. Bill then played the video one frame at a time and we gasped. The mist seemed to be floating and we could make out a ghostly apparition seemingly reaching out with a ghoulish head and outstretched arm; almost crying out. When we replayed the video at normal speed in was unnoticeable.

Chapter Twenty-Nine

'a breath of fresh air'

Smokers were a continual problem. I really can't see the logic when some of them would say that they like to stay in non-smoking properties such as ours. Why for fuck's sake? We set the business up so that people like us, non-smokers, could stay somewhere and not have some stupid prick puffing away and allowing smoke to stink the place out.

When we were on holidays in Tasmania, just before we bought Ormiston, we stayed at a motel at Bicheno on the east coast of Tassie. When we opened the door of the unit the smell almost knocked us out. We immediately opened all the windows and front and rear doors, but the fresh air did nothing. The smell had got into the fabrics and was, quite frankly, nauseating. I went back to reception to arrange a new room, but the receptionist said they were full and there were no other rooms available. Being late in the day and during peak holiday season we did not feel like driving off to find another place to stay so we put up with it. We left our gear in the car and went for a walk and dinner while giving the sea breeze an opportunity to air the unit and reduce the stink. It only worked to a small degree and by the morning we all had sore throats and watery eyes. I have no doubt some smokers realise the damage their damn habit is doing to rooms and dwellings and that is why they prefer to stay in sweet smelling non-smoking properties.

One of the troubles is that when they suck in their last desperate breaths of toxic smouldering vegetation in the garden before they butt out, they walk in the house breathing and wheezing expelling their smoke laden breath in the house. In addition, their clothing smells of smoke and that contributes to their smoking odour following them through the house. In many cases I have noticed other non-smoking house guests sniffing the air in disgust as they pick up the odour floating in the air. Invariably when we service a room after a smoking house guests has departed, we have to air it for the rest of the day and spray Febreze on the fabrics to freshen the room up; and this is without them actually smoking in the room. Just being there creates a bad odour. What I can say without fear of contradiction is that they are a dying race.

We had a note on each mantlepiece in the bedrooms reminding them that this is a smoke free house and if you must smoke then do so in the garden and away from open windows and the veranda. I used to chuckle when they would be walking around the garden in the rain braving the elements, coughing and gasping. When they returned to the house, I would make a point of saying "popped out for a bit of fresh air did you?" With a broad smile on my face. Most smile and nod. Others look at me with a vacant look as if to say, "how did you know".

I had an Asian guest who started smoking in his room but because the air-conditioning has two large intake ducts in the hallway it draws air out from under the doors of the rooms and so any smell of smoke can be detected in the passageways. I nabbed him quick smart.

I have been mistaken at times and thought I smelt smoke which, in fact, can be from a smoker coming back into the house. (I wonder if they realise how much they carry the smell of smoke on their clothes and themselves.)

On this particular day I could swear that someone was smoking in the room, so I got down and stuck my nose under the door. Suddenly, the door opened, and I kept going along the passageway and looked up and said, "just checking for silverfish". I should have tapped on the wall and said I was checking the walls!!

Some smoking guests think they are being smart by leaning out of the window and having a puff. I've caught a few with my 'ultra-sensitive' nose. They don't realise that air gets drawn into the house through windows, rather than the opposite, so the smell and smoke penetrates into the room and the house anyway.

One day we had a young lady climb out of the window into the atrium outside one of the rooms. Little did she realise that our laundry was on the other side of the wall and I had an access doorway from the laundry into the atrium. I leaped into the atrium and she nearly did herself an embarrassment, but I got my point across. One very embarrassed girl, but it is amazing the extremes smokers will go to have a crafty smoke. More amazing is that they don't realise how obvious and easily they are to catch out. The fact is that smoking stinks and I have just the nose for it.

We did have one grumpy guest who insisted in smoking on the veranda and I ticked him off a couple of times. However, he was a serial pest and repeat offender. He was staying 2 nights and he was by himself. That I can understand as I can't imagine who would want to go on holiday with the prick. He went on one of the cruise boats and once again tried to smoke in the enclosed areas and was cautioned by the staff. He then proceeded to the open deck area and being the 'fat slob' he was slammed down onto a chair and broke one of the chair legs off and then threatened the staff that he was going to sue them. The crew dealt with him as politely as they could and asked where he was staying and refunded his cruise ticket to quieten him down. When the cruise company phoned me to tell me what had happened, I told them he was being difficult here as well. Fortunately, he had booked through a wholesaler, so I called them to say he was being a difficult guest and asked where he was staying next. I then phoned that property and warned them what to expect. Shit happens but these difficult people don't realise that we have our own jungle drum and when we get dishonest or difficult guests, we have the ability to inform other properties on the itinerary. Since the advent of emails and the internet it is not unusual to either send or receive messages about problematic guests.

Just recently we were having lunch in one of the outdoor dining areas on the Strahan waterfront. Absolutely magnificent day. There was a cycling race arriving within the next few hours and not by design there were about a hundred motor-cycle riders in town at the same time. The town centre and the waterfront were a hive of activity. We had ordered our food and a group of 5 bikers came after we ordered and sat at the next table. One of them was finishing off a rollie weed smoke but I just observed as he was being discreet (sneaky in fact) but the smoke was minimal. However, we were in a non-smoking, eating area. I kept an eye on him. Our food arrived and we started munching and as I was finishing, I noticed another biker light up. Now these were fairly hefty guys, a couple in leathers. I called out "excuse me guys, this is a non-smoking area and people are eating." Both offenders quickly stubbed out with a couple of snarly looks but nothing else was said. I noticed conversation on the table was muted after my interjection. Sometimes you need to speak up. Probably the most disappointing aspect was that one of the staff members of the establishment did not mention anything to them even though there were packets of cigarettes on the table. I have a view that there are very few bad staff just bad managers. When a staff member is clearly not carrying out their duties correctly then I would look to the manager or supervisor for the responsibility of ensuring that staff carry out their work appropriately. When managers and supervisors do their job then it will flow through to the junior staff that require their superiors to guide them. Now and again you will get staff that do not respond to training and if so, get rid of them.

Chapter Thirty

'I booked a room with water views'

I can't believe it. This happened a few years ago and it was a first in 17 years. I was just finishing some garden spraying and said "hi" to a couple of guests heading out for a walk along the foreshore. I could hear a vehicle coming up the driveway, but I kept going as I knew Carolyn was inside and she would look after any house guest checking in.

It was a couple, Carolyn seemed to think they were European but spoke very good English and driving a small motor home. He stopped in the car park and walked in through the guest entrance on the side of the house and Carolyn met him as he was walking down the hallway. He said, "just thought I would let you know that I will be parking in your driveway for a while and I'll also be using your Wi-Fi."

"Did you tell him to fuck off?" I asked.

"No of course not," she said, "but I did tell him that the parking area was for house guests and that if he wanted to go online then he should go around to the internet café."

"Well I wouldn't have been so polite," I said, "the bloody cheek...do you mean to say that he expected to come into a private property and use their internet and then buggar off and

say thanks very much. Where do these people get the idea that when they are on holiday that everything should be free?"

In fact, motor home and caravan people are the worst. They expect to be able to park their vans wherever they like, expect councils to provide free camping areas and never a care about the caravan parks and the hard-working park owners who provide great facilities and are trying to make a living. They even drive into the caravan park expecting to use their bathrooms and toilets for free while they park 50 metres down the road in a shopping centre car park for the night. What is wrong with these fucking people. We were quick to secure the WiFi with a password.

It is like some of the sticky beakers we get who walk around the garden, onto the verandas and peak into the guest bedrooms. I have lost count of the times I have had to say, "excuse me but people are in their bedrooms and this is a private residence." "Oh," they say, "it's a B & B and you're open to the public."

"Yes, but only if you stay here."

"No difference." They say.

On one occasion I said, "tell me, when you are at home do you walk into private residences and B & Bs in your home-town and peer into their bedrooms."

"No,"

"Then why the fuck are you doing it here?"

Vacant look on their face and they go off in a huff grumbling about unfriendly tourism operators.

"We had one guest come out and say "Someone was just standing at my bedroom window looking in." Then I would explain. Apparently, our guests can see how fundamentally stupid these people are. I might add that the perpetrators are usually people who stay in the cheapest accommodation they can find and would not dream of staying in a place of our standard. Thank god! Then we would have to put up with them for a couple of days...as I said previously 'thank goodness most of our guests are our sort of people!'

There was a night in the restaurant that all seven tables were full. We had some house guests and a few from outside. As was our custom we would suggest that in between courses, if they would like, they could view our history room and on fine nights go up to our widow's walk and enjoy the sunset.

On this one night, during our first two years of operation, two Aussie guys came down from the gallery and commented on our collection of photographs of ships that frequented Macquarie Harbour from the 1880's until quite recently. They enquired about the ship that was sunk by the USS Snapper near Yokohama during WW2 and were curious how an Australian/NZ ship was sunk by an American submarine off Japan. The fact was that the old coastal trader had been bought by a Japanese company well before WW2. However jokingly, and without any malice, I said "Oh, you know the yanks; they'll blow anything out of the water." Then I realised that there was an elderly retired American stockbroker and his wife, who were staying with us, sitting on the table behind me. The Aussie guys laughed as I retreated to the kitchen.

I rushed into the kitchen and put my hands over my head and said "God, what have I just done?" Carolyn asked me what had happened. The entire kitchen broke into laughter. I said to Carolyn "You'll have to do that section, I'm too embarrassed."

"Don't worry," she replied, "they're both as deaf as posts. They won't have heard a word you said."

Thank god!

Ever wondered what goes through the minds of hospitality staff when confronted with rude or stupid patrons? For example, take a rude diner at a restaurant. I recall this happened at a restaurant about 20 years ago owned by an industry associate. I was told the story by one of our house guests who was there at the time. Our house guest was staying at the establishment which also operates a restaurant on premises. He was standing on the veranda next to the main entrance that was also the entrance to the in-house restaurant. A red Porsche pulls up and parks right at the front steps effectively blocking the entrance for anyone else. The two occupants of the Porsche step out and leave the car blocking the entrance. Our house guests says, "don't you think you should move your car?" The driver looks at him, grunts and then ignores his request and walks into the restaurant. Our house guest commented that the number plate was NAVY. When he told me the story I said, "that would be bloody right, a naval officer."

The Porsche driver was abrupt and rude to the waiter and after ordering their meal, soup was brought out to their table which he complained was not hot. The owner of the establishment, who is also the chef, walked out and said to the diner, "Look, obviously we are not going to make you happy tonight so please leave." Loud enough so everyone in the restaurant could hear. The couple then walked out to a low roar of approval from the other guests. I bumped into the owner a short while ago at my sister's 60th birthday and we had a laugh about it together with a few adjectives that he did not use on the guest.

You see as much as you would like to say exactly what is on your mind it is far better to bite one's tongue. Letting rip with a tirade will often exacerbate the situation and things can get out of hand all too easily.

In situations such as the bad-mannered Porsche driver the waiter would go back to the kitchen and probably say, "We have a total tosser on table five; I think we are going to have a problem." Instead of saying "Look sir you're behaving like a total dickhead, you're annoying other guests so do us all a favour and fuck off." He is politely told to leave, of course, as only a true professional would do. Sometimes it is better to politely request they leave, leaving them in no doubt what you, and neighbouring diners, are really thinking. Depending on their IQ I guess.

A friend of ours just called in while I am writing so I thought I would include this little snippet of wonder. Our friend owns a waterfront restaurant and accommodation. He has eight units all with water views of some description. A guy checked in this afternoon and upon the staff showing him to his room he complained about no water views.

"But you have water views," said the staff member.

"No, I haven't," argued the customer.

"The water is just there," pointed out the staff member.

"I want another room with better water views."

"The other rooms are booked."

"Well I booked a room with water views and that's what I want."

"But the water is there."

"But there's a big tree right in front."

"I'm sorry sir the other rooms are taken."

"Well get me the manager."

I know this property well and all the rooms have good water views and yes, there are trees as well, but you can see the water through and around them and the units are only a few metres from the water's edge.

As soon as our friend gets the message and the staff member explains the situation he goes straight to the shed and gets his chainsaw and a ladder. He shinnies up the ladder and chops down the offending part of the tree. I guess that is customer service ...bending over backwards to please the 'buggars'. He calls out to the guy looking out from his balcony...

"Can you see the water now?"

Now you would think that after the tree came down that would be the end of it. Next minute he was down at reception; apparently, he had locked his keys in his car. Suddenly everyone realised what the problem was. He was a dickhead.

Einstein said, "Two things are infinite: the universe and human stupidity; and I'm not sure about the universe."

I am also reminded of another saying, "Better to remain silent and have people think you a fool than open your mouth and have it confirmed."

It would come as no surprise to readers that conversations between two people may not actually articulate the words in the minds of those involved. The question I pose is 'do we actually say what we are thinking?' I think not. I suppose that if one is totally pure of thought then articulating those thoughts into words would not be a problem. Others not so pure of mind (I include myself in this category) would need to translate profane thoughts and emotions into more acceptable speech. When this does not occur then this is when we will hear all sorts of obscene and profane language most likely in the form of argument (or jokes). In some cases, there are people for whom profanity is their preferred method of discourse.

In hospitality the use of profanity is widespread. Many employees are young and for them the language is more commonly used it would seem. However widespread profanity is restricted to back of house between employees and as an industry standard courtesy, politeness and good diction is not only encouraged but essential when dealing with customers.

Chapter Thirty-One

'one nip or three and other indiscretions'

We made a bold statement with our provision of liquor. We called our bar and lounge the Port 'o Call to capture the atmosphere of life at sea during the time when the house was built. It was also the time of Strahan becoming an important gateway to the west of Tasmania for the mining of gold, silver and copper. I designed the bar and gave the drawings to a cabinet maker and the result speaks for itself. The bar was stocked with the finest selection of spirits and liquors together with a cellar stocked with a choice of over 100 different wines. Guests would be encouraged to inspect the cellar and select their wines if they chose to do so. For most of our time at Ormiston I operated the bar each evening and for the eight years we operated the in-house restaurant 'Fredericks'. After we closed the restaurant in 2004, we continued to provide beverages for our guests.

At any time, the guests would be able to partake of a beverage and if myself, Carolyn or any of the staff were not close by then there was a sign asking them to ring the bell at the office door and we would magically appear to render assistance. Most of the time this system worked well. On odd occasions we would be faced with a guest popping behind the bar and helping themselves. As any publican will tell you, that is a definite no-no. In fact, a quick way to piss your host off as well as a contravention of the Liquor and Gaming Act. I am surprised even to this day that some small licensed accommodation establishments provide what is called an 'honour bar' whereby the guest helps themselves and makes a notation on a docket, pad or 'bar book' with their purchase. In my view, and emphatically confirmed by some of our 'honest guests', a quick way to lose money on liquor sales. Even without providing an honour bar some will quickly nip behind the bar and throw a good proportion of spirit in their glass and then deftly mention that "you weren't around old chap and I didn't want to disturb you, so I added a single nip." Single nip my fucking arse! The temptation is just too great for some guests. They have the option of using a jigger to measure the nip, but most will either not use it or chose to overspill when pouring. They also pour two nips and enter one. I have observed this in action at another establishment. Unbeknown to the guest behind the bar, I was observing his fraudulent behaviour which included taking three beers from the fridge and entering two in the book. I simply chose to correct his quantities instead of causing a scene. I then recommended to the owner that he reconsider his bar operation. Removing a guest from behind the bar happened on occasions and I am sure some got away with helping themselves. I recall asking Carolyn if she had recently sold any great grandfather port. She replied perhaps one or two nips in the past few weeks. I replied that I have not sold any and half the fucking bottle has disappeared. 'Honour Bar', forget it the bastards will rob you blind.

The downside of cleaning rooms

Oh! Give me strength. If it wasn't bad enough to do people's laundry it is fucking awful to find lumps of shit on your hands as you go to put them in the washing machine. We started off going to every length to ensure our guests had an unforgettable experience. From our perspective we wanted to set the bar high so that we were talked about and recommended at every level. To do that we were going to have to put a lot of pressure on ourselves, but we were prepared to go to extremes to make the business work and do stuff that other properties either did not think necessary or frankly did not want to do themselves.

"Complimentary laundry," said Carolyn. So that was it, off we went. Most of the time it went well. Provided we got the washing in early in the day, we could have it back the next morning in time for departure if they were only in for the one night. During those first few years we got an outside laundry to do the bed linen and towels which just left incidentals to do in our laundry. Of course, we had to factor in that we were on the west coast of Tasmania and if the laundry did not get delivered for some reason, especially in winter, we had to have plenty of back up. So invariably at least once a week we would need to wash and dry our own linen and towels. Then there were the returns of laundry that were either not washed properly or were torn or frayed. Then our towels started coming back in a bad state of repair and needing to be replaced so we started doing our own as we had colour coordinated bathroom accessories and it was getting expensive to replace missing or damaged items. We also had expensive bed linen and that was starting to show wear and tear from the commercial laundry. We tried using their laundry bed linen, but the standard was too crap. Then another disgruntled accommodation property in Strahan decided to install a commercial laundry and asked us to participate and that went well until Parks and Wildlife decided to do a controlled burn off behind their property which quickly became uncontrolled and the fire burnt down the laundry as well as the storage shed for the town Christmas decorations. The mayor at the time bravely tried to save some gear and got his eyebrows singed for his gallant effort.

It wasn't long before we were doing our own laundry. With two machines and two dryers we found we could cater for our five rooms easily. Carolyn supervised of course and when the staff went home, she would finish off. If it was a fine day, and there were more than people think on the west coast, then the linen and towels got some fresh air as well. Back to guest laundry. Most of the house guests were appreciative and cooperative. Some were not. Some would completely empty their suitcases and dump it outside their bedroom door. Some would even expect it the next morning when they dumped it in the evening before. So, then Carolyn wrote a note for the rooms and included a shopping size bag to limit the amount of laundry. Most of the time that worked. The guests now had instructions and a bag to put it in. For some it was just too damn fucking difficult and we would get a knock on the office door in the evening with the guest holding a bundle of laundry for us to do for the next morning. It was then time to ensure we gave verbal instructions as well when we checked them in, just in case they were terminally stupid.

I suppose we got to the 'fuck this' stage after a middle-aged couple from UK stayed. At first meeting they seemed very pleasant and Carolyn must have been away as I checked them in and recall having a fair degree of contact with them. My first recoil of horror was when I took them to the room and as I was explaining our facilities, he opened his mouth, it may have been a smile, and he had a mouth full of rotten teeth. I nearly threw up as his breath was putrid. Outwardly appearances can be so deceptive. I quickly withdrew. They had breakfast the next morning, and went on a cruise on the Gordon River. Jan, our housekeeper, went in to service the room as I passed by and said looks like there is a bag of laundry here. They had conveniently put the laundry in the bag and left it outside the door. So, I grabbed the bag and took it out to the laundry area. Now Carolyn would not start guest laundry until the house laundry was done and she would usually strip the beds before Jan got in. However, when there is only one of us doing breakfast and other morning duties, or should I say when I am doing it solo, I don't go into the rooms before Jan starts. So, I decide to do the guest laundry first, so I pick up the bag from the Christina room and start pulling it out of the bag directly into the machine. Urrrghh! I got a handful of shit. I quickly threw the lot into the laundry sink whereby I observed that both his and her underwear were full of squashed turds. Luckily, I am not squeamish, so I put them into a bucket and took them out to one of our back-room toilets and hung them in the bowl while flushing it at the same time until the underwear was decent enough to put in the washing machine.

Now in this industry we see more than our share of skid marks and other nasties. It makes you wonder how people can live like this. If I had an accident I would bloody well clean it up myself instead of putting it in a laundry bag for the guesthouse to clean up. How in the world do the both of them crap in their pants on the same day and leave it there or is this a daily activity? Maybe they got a dose of the runs or a bug, but the least they could do was wash the fucking lumps out of their undies. The strangest thing about this incident is that they did not blink an eyelid when they returned from their day's excursion. It was as if nothing had happened. I would be mortified if I had done something like this. It is not as if they were geriatric, they seemed to be fairly 'fit and active'. Too bloody active as it turned out.

I mentioned this incident to another accommodation property in Strahan a few days later and she said you were lucky. She had to recently change some of the curtains in one of her units as there was excrement on them. She said it was as if someone had gone along the curtains wiping their backside until it was clean. She said it was a family who stayed there but they must have known as the unit smelled terrible when she went in to clean it. These incidents might be the exception but nevertheless they really knock you around when they happen. When the guest leaves and they have paid cash how can you charge them a cleaning fee.

Back to our guest laundry again. It was after this incident that we decided to charge for laundry. It was either that or not provide any guest laundry service and as we did not have a separate laundry just for guests the decision was obvious. We started off with a $5 fee for washing and drying and at the same time providing a calico bag in which to place the washing. Frequently the guests would cram in as much in as they could and even then, pile more on top of the bag. We put up with this for a few months and then decided that we would charge $10.00 a bag thus allowing for the excess amount. It seemed to do the trick. No-one questioned the price and we were happy to cover the extra loads at times. To think that we offered a free service for those first few years allowing our wonderful guests to take full advantage and give us a bit of shit along the way.

It wasn't just free laundry that we provided in the first few years. During breakfast I used to go out and give the cars a summary hose down and a bit of a wash if they were exceptionally dirty. The guests, in fact, were really surprised and appreciative and it also helped when we had visiting travel agents and staff from Tasmania's Temptations Holidays. When asked, by guests and others, why I was doing it I used to say that the dirty cars were making the car park look shabby and bringing the tone of the property down. After all the house itself was as 'pretty as a picture' and cars covered in dirt and road grime did detract from the overall vista. It didn't last though, after a few years of doing it I gave it a miss and put some car cleaning equipment next to the car park hose. Surprisingly many of them took up the hose and sponge. What pissed me off though was the fact that in most cases they couldn't be bothered coiling the hose back up and would just throw it over the garden bed and rose bushes. I purchased an auto coil hose so that it would retract automatically. That worked for a while until a few of them must have pulled it past the safe point and broke the internal return mechanism and we were back where we started. It is very hard to find something that is guest proof. The buggars will find some way of breaking it eventually.

Pets!

You know some guests can be downright sneaky. Not long after we opened, we had two couples staying with us. They paid for two rooms and initially all seemed well. I was in the garden and noticed that there was a dog in the car. Shortly after that the guests opened the car and took the dog for a walk. When they returned, I mentioned that we did not allow pets in the house and they said quite all right as the dog would sleep in the car. I took them at their word. In the morning, about 6am, I was in the breakfast room setting up for breakfast and opposite one of the guest rooms. The door opened and the guest went out the side door of the house holding something wrapped in a blanket. I was looking out of one of the windows in the breakfast room and could see him place the blanket on the ground covering their dog, about the size of a Labrador, and then putting the dog in the car. He then returned to the room. They had obviously had the dog in their room overnight. Some properties do allow pets, but we were not one of them and they knew that. There were a couple of accommodation properties in Strahan that allowed pets but no, they would prefer to stay with us and sneak the dog in. In this case luckily there were no accidents and no smells to clean up. Another example of guests being dishonest. I could have been confrontational had it not been after the event, so nothing was to be gained and they were checking out that morning.   However, it still stuck in my craw that they intended to put one over us.

Dirty bedlinen

Suffice to say that the general public do any number of things in beds.   Most of the time this would fit into the normal category including spills and accidents.   At times there are incidents that could be termed 'close encounters of the fourth kind'.   I am not going to go there so sorry if that disappoints anyone.   There are just some incidents when you had to have been there, or in this case would have preferred not to have been there.   Our housekeepers deserve a medal.

Did you turn the lights out?

We had a young chap from the UK arrive one afternoon. He filled in his registration card and I noticed he wrote Midsomer Norton as the town in his address. I asked him if he turned out the light when he left, you must be the last person left there alive. He looked at me and laughed and said he has had plenty of comments whilst in Australia. The area in the television series is fictional and is filmed in Oxfordshire and Buckinghamshire and based on Caroline Graham's novels; Midsomer Norton is actually in Somerset.

The Italian professor

We had an Italian Professor staying with us. Polite enough when he checked in. When he came in for dinner, I greeted him and showed him to a table. I said, "how are you this evening, did you enjoy your day in the wilderness?" he said, "it's none of your business how I am and what I do." The other houseguests on the adjacent tables were gobsmacked, they sat there with their mouths open aghast at his rudeness. I wanted to say, "well get fucked then." But I didn't. I looked at the other houseguests with a "what the fuck" expression and went into the kitchen and said to Carolyn "you can serve that rude Italian prick." I ignored the bastard for the rest of his stay. Now who knows why he said that and why he was so rude. I'm not a fucking psychologist. He obviously had shit on his liver for some reason and wanted nothing to do with me. Luckily Carolyn and I could bounce off each other and avoid further confrontation, but I would have preferred to tell him to pack his fucking bags and go somewhere else.

Chapter Thirty-two

'Chefs, noisy kitchens and trainees'

When we set out the plan of the house for the restoration we had to decide if the kitchen was going to remain in the same place or we would relocate it to another location within the house. After some debate we decided it should remain where it was. We would, of course, rip it to pieces and start with a shell for a new fit out.

The location was at the end of the west wing of the house and we had two bedrooms in that same corridor. At the opposite end of the corridor were the dining rooms so we would have to walk past the two bedrooms between the kitchen and dining rooms. We decided that would not be a problem because, in all likelihood, the occupants of the bedrooms would be in the dining rooms anyway; we were concerned about traffic and noise and all said and done, we were primarily an accommodation business.

Considering the layout of the house and the proximity of kitchen to bedrooms we were very mindful of the noise factor. This aspect of our business was taken up by the minister of finance, fun and laughter, Carolyn. I was more than happy for Carolyn to have custody of both kitchen and staff management within her portfolio. During the restoration and immediately following, my responsibility was bricks and mortar, garden, repair and maintenance and the ever-increasing presence of technology. In partnership we both attended to the needs of the guests and my role was to jointly engage with meet and greets and manage the bar and cellar, wine lists and drink service for guests. In addition, we had the office to manage so Carolyn managed the accounts and I looked after statistics. To some this may seem a little over the top for a B&B guesthouse but from a business perspective it held us in good stead for the tough times ahead.

In the course of the removal of effects we had a number of near new white melamine bench height floor cupboards which I had been using in the garage for storage at the Brisbane house. They would make ideal cupboards in the new kitchen together with new stainless-steel benches. The inventory of the kitchen was a new Garland Starfire gas six burner cooktop and oven, two stainless steel free standing bench units, stainless steel bench with three sinks, dishwasher, microwave, industrial range hood and extraction unit, three door glass fronted refrigerator unit, large chest freezer and our domestic fridge and freezer from our kitchen in Brisbane. The above was supplemented by an array of pots, pans and utensils from the hotel and catering supply who like other suppliers was most appreciative of our custom. At the same time, once again, we were amazed at our naivety in the capital needed to furnish an accommodation and restaurant.

From the outset our restaurant would be fine dining. In that respect Carolyn already had an extensive array of fine china and silver cutlery. This was supplemented with more of the same including antique silverware where appropriate. The dining room crockery was all royal Doulton so initially we ensured we had a minimum of twenty of each item. In addition, Carolyn also had an extensive collection of

Wedgewood crockery. Our collection of Waterford and Stuart crystal also helped raise the bar in the service of alcohol. The downside of all these expensive items was when one got broken, which happened with some regularity. Rob was our first chef and we read the riot act to him regarding kitchen noise and care of china. In most respects Rob complied. On first employing him we trialled him with a three-course meal and invited our new house manager Jodi to join us. After the meal the four of us would sit down and review the food and presentation as if we were guests. Jodi arrived in a bit of a panic as her live-in boyfriend was a bit apprehensive about the foursome arrangement. I got the impression that our new chef Rob had a bit of a reputation with the ladies. Before the evening was over Jodi left after a phone call from her boyfriend who was going to come around to the house and punch the chef's lights out if she didn't come home immediately. It was touch and go for a while whether Jodi would stay as her fisherman boyfriend, as well as being the jealous type, was also pretty good with his fists. As it turned out I spoke to Jodi's boyfriend shortly after the incident and assured him that all was above board and he was welcome at any time to call into the house. Some years later Jodi and Michael got married at Ormiston House and they now have two lovely children.

The kitchen needed to be inspected by the local food inspector who just happened to be Jodi's father. I might add there were no favours and we complied with all requests and got our certificate of compliance. We opened with three rooms and for the first month we were restricted to just serving house guests as our approval to be open to the public had not yet been approved by Council. Apparently, there was some grey area regarding zoning. We could have a wildlife park on the property but not a restaurant; go figure. The outcome of that decision was that we were granted dispensation. We could also be open to the public as we only had seven tables, three of which would be occupied by house guests. Thankfully there were no objections from other dining establishments, and it was full steam ahead.

As a team we ensured that the kitchen remained as quiet as was possible. The banging and clashing of pots and pans were kept to a minimum but working on the stainless-steel benches was noisy and mostly unavoidable. We did minimise some of the noise by the positioning of towels on some of the surfaces and this worked well. The opening and closing of the kitchen door during service was an issue. The door itself was the old back door as the kitchen was an add on during the 1960s. It did have some heavy glass panelling and, due to its solid construction, it did muffle quite a lot of the regular kitchen noise. During service one person would carry the plates while another would carefully open and close the door for them. This worked for us and for the most part kept the guests happy.

There were incidents from time to time, especially after service when we were cleaning up, when we would get a knock on the kitchen door. This also annoyed us as we had a bell for service on the office door which was directly alongside the kitchen. Despite the fact we had a note on the office door to say "please ring this bell if you need us" they would still knock on the kitchen door. This continued for the whole twenty-one years that we were there. What is wrong with these fucking people. We would politely say "please ring the bell if you need us as we may not be in the kitchen." They would say "but we didn't like to ring the bell." We would say "if you don't ring the bell, we may not hear you." What I wanted to say was "For fuck's sake, we put the fucking bell there for you to fucking ring it, so we could fucking hear it if you fucking needed us." But I didn't.

In the end if we had guests back in the F O Henry and Amelia rooms early in the evening we would minimise the clean-up in the kitchen to essential food safety, fill and run the dishwasher as quietly as we could, stack and soak the pots and pans in the large sink and leave the noisy work until the morning.

Trainees

Ahh yes, we have had a few of those. They come out of VET in schools or the hospitality college and join us for a bit of part time work or work experience and in most cases had trouble making beds and pouring wines. We try to ease them into the work gently but only a few stuck it out for a season. We did have one girl who showed promise. Her mother even came down with her. Friends of ours even agreed to rent a room for her in their house. Her work ethic was reasonable and initially we thought there was a lot of promise.

It all got complicated when she and the husband started bonking in the house where she rented the room. Then the husband got shitty because the trainee started bonking the guy in the house next door to the house where she was renting a room and at the same time still bonking the husband. The guy in the next house had a fiancée and so she got the shits and moved out. Then the wife in the house where the trainee was renting a room left her husband. The husband and the trainee decided they would leave town as well so we lost a trainee and friends because the wife thought we should have known what was going on.

Then a private detective came to see us because the husband had acquired a boat and hadn't paid for it and wanted to know where he was. Then we heard that the trainee sold her car to an old couple for cash but didn't tell them that it was under finance so the finance company repossessed the car leaving the old couple without their cash and their car and the husband and the trainee then went to the mainland and no one had heard from them since. So that was the last trainee we employed.

We did have a couple of young housekeepers that did not last long in fact one of them lasted 4 hours with me. I firstly gave her the royal tour, introduced her to the regular housekeeper who she was going to assist. The regular housekeeper took her through the room cleaning and set up and then gave her a room to service. I popped my head in after about an hour and nothing was being done. The new girl said she was trying but she was having a bad day. I said but you haven't done anything yet. Then she said, "I have a lot of personal problems" and I said, "well go home and when you have sorted your problems out come back, you can't bring you own problems into work." She left in tears and we never saw her again. As I said before, I am not a fucking psychologist. What are we supposed to do with some of these young people? Stop everything and sit down with them for the next 4 hours while we listen to all the crap going on in their lives; close the business down because someone has a 'personal problem'. FFS.

Chapter Thirty-three

'you just had to be there'

Bedroom athletics

I often read about rock stars who trash rooms but thankfully that never happened to us. We had many celebrities stay with us and all, without exception, left the rooms in the same state in which they arrived. There have been, however, some careless individuals along the way who have totally amazed me by their absolute fucking stupidity.

Shortly after we opened in 1995, we had a couple stay in our Mary Alice room and at one stage she obviously intended on having a plunge in the antique Victorian clawfoot bath in their en-suite. Nothing wrong with that although it would be a good idea to turn the taps off at some stage and not forget and leave them running until the bathroom is totally flooded and running onto the carpet in the bedroom. There was a drain in the centre of the bathroom but unknown to us at the time there was an inclination in the floor that allowed some of the water to accumulate and run back towards the bedroom. The hot water must have been running for a while because it drained the hot water storage system so that other guests had to wait for a hot shower or bath. Of course, when the other guests complained I thought we had a fault in the hot water system. I am crawling around in the roof at night trying to find the fault. It was only as I apologised to the guests that the lady in question told me that they had a little flood.

It was not long after we finished bringing our fifth room online that upon the departure of the guests, I found that the brass taps and faucet in the Christina room, above the spa, were bent downwards. I did recall that the previous evening, after a young couple had checked in, a lot of noise, gasping and splashing of a sexual nature coming from the room. Under these circumstances one beats a hasty retreat and tried not to think too much about the activities being undertaken. My assessment the following morning during service was that one of the activities being undertaken the previous evening was performed whilst standing on the brass tapware. Whilst it must have been uncomfortable and possibly a dangerous position, I have no doubt that the persons in question didn't give one iota of consideration to the fact that they were buggaring up the hardware... (poor choice of words there). How do we, the owners, reconcile with this travesty of trust. Call them up and tell them that during their period of sexual athleticism that they have totally fucked up the waterworks in the spa. Send them a bill for "plumber to fix damage caused by 'over-fucking' frivolities". Inform them that taps are for turning the water on and not for balancing delicately and holding on to the shower rose for support while being administered any number of the 245 positions in the Kama Sutra. I fully understand why our housekeeper used to cringe sometimes, poor girl.

The Christina room was our room for lovers and of that we had no doubt. The spa bath and water views were very popular. One middle aged couple stayed with us and during breakfast the following morning, after his wife left the table, asked me if there were any complaints about his guitar playing. I said, 'not to my knowledge', upon which he informed me that he and his wife had a lovely evening with her in the spa bath and him playing his guitar sitting on the edge of the bar totally naked. I told him that I was glad he enjoyed the evening. What else could I say?

In my view the unsung heroes of hospitality are the cleaning staff and housekeeping. Without them there would not be a tourism or hospitality industry and though they work behind the scenes and not often acknowledged they literally deserve a medal for the tasks they need to carry out. Whenever we are on holiday, we make a point of saying hello and thanking them for the service they provide.

The same must be said about the waitering staff in eateries and cafes. They silently put up with some atrocious behaviour by some patrons. We salute you.

Mining function

One of our early clients was a large mining company who approached us not too long after we opened. This is the same company I mentioned previously where we stuffed up the order of service. We received a request from the mining company to accommodate them for a Christmas function for the senior management and shift supervisors in the mine. Of course, we were delighted to host the function for about 20 personnel. Ordinarily we would be a little cautious with miners as just like sailors they can be a rowdy bunch after a few drinks. On this occasion the senior management would be there, and we already knew some of the executive as they had dined with us previously. All went well for the first couple of hours until one of the mine supervisors got too drunk. Apparently, he had a few drinks before arriving and was under the weather when he arrived. During the course of the evening we got a knock on the kitchen door with the mine superintendent holding a twisted brass fireguard and screen from one of the fireplaces. This particular employee had fallen over into the fireplace and virtually crushed the polished brass screen. The superintendent apologised profusely and said he would take it away and get his metal workers to fix it and return it in good condition or replace it if it was beyond repair. We were OK with that and he promised to keep the group under control. This is par for the course in any drinking establishment and accidents do happen. The evening proceeded until we got another knock on the door to apologise further as the same employee had now vomited in the toilet. The superintendent was mortified and apologised once again profusely saying "no-one throws up at Ormiston House." The offending miner was then told to leave by the bosses and as he stumbled down the steps, he fell against one of the 'fleur de les' concrete flowerpots, cracking it at the base. I was now not impressed. I went back to the store room to get the mop and bucket only to be met by the senior executives who grabbed the cleaning gear and whilst apologising profusely started cleaning up the vomit in the toilet insisting that we charge them a hefty cleaning bill in compensation.

It would be no surprise to say that they did not do another staff party at our premises, but they did continue with the executive dinners and drinks. From our perspective a little inconvenient but very profitable and happy not to have another staff function.

Flags got pinched and the fence got burnt

It was with absolute pride and pleasure that we designed our own house flag to fly from the masthead above the tower. The cost of having a custom-made flag was not so pleasurable but this was costed within our start up budget. We also had a free-standing flagpole with yardarms in the front garden where we flew the Australian flag, the Tasmanian state flag and a smaller house flag. What we did not budget for was the wild west coast weather which blew like a bastard and even the military grade bunting could not stand the blustering for more than 12 months. All up the cost of the 2 custom made flags and the state and national flags were over $1000 and during those early days we were trying to minimise the costs. So as soon as the flags got a bit tatty and after Carolyn had tidied the edges we were still faced with an annual replacement. We shopped around and would you believe that it was significantly cheaper going through a flag business in Sydney rather than going through a Tasmanian supplier. Initially we always gave Tasmanian suppliers the opportunity of getting our business, but they had to be competitive. After all we were not a bloody charity. It was soon becoming apparent that regardless of the commodity we had to shop around if we were to contain our costs. We decided that in future we would further embrace the Scottish heritage of Ormiston House by flying a Scottish flag. We decided that the Royal Standard of Scotland, or Lion Rampant, would be more colourful and appropriate than the Saltire or St Andrews Cross and significantly cheaper than our custom-made house flag. In addition, our new supplier could supply the smaller flags for the front garden flagpole at a reduced cost and improved quality so that arrangement remained in situ for a number of years. Repair and replacement were still required, but not so frequently. Our supplier, John Vaughan, advised us that he had designed a flag that we may be interested in to replace the Lion Rampant. It was the flag of the Scottish Australian Heritage Council a symbol of the unity between Australia and Scotland and of the bond we shared. We were most pleased to fly this flag as we knew it also represented the original founding family of Strahan, the Henry's.

All was well and for quite a few years the flags flew with absolute majesty until a few of the local teenagers decided it would be a good lark to pinch our flags from the front flagpole. One morning I came out and the flags and lanyards were missing. I was pissed off to say the least. I called the local constabulary, made out the report and waited for the resultant investigation. It was not long before one of the constables returned with a bag containing some lanyards and one Tasmanian state flag. He said that he had spoken to 'a number of likely suspects' and was I going to take it further and press charges. As this is a small community, I declined saying I would leave it up to the local police to speak with any offenders and that it would be better if I did not know them. However, I never did replace the flags or fly them again from that flagpole. The pole was in a vulnerable position and at that stage we did not have any security cameras. That was until I got a phone call early one morning from an industry associate who was walking his dog to come out and see our front fence. When I went to the front gate I looked at where the front fence had been and most of it was missing. I went around the side of the house and a large section of that side was missing as well. By this stage some of the locals had passed by and there was quite a few gathering outside our house. The locals were horrified that there had been such a violation of such a revered home. Of most dismay to me was that the fence was a historic fence built by the original owner and made of Huon pine, Celery Top pine and King Billy pine.

The police were once again called, this time it was the local sergeant and I could see by the look on his face he knew who he would be calling on. Apparently, there was a big party the previous night on the beach not far away and during the night they had a large bonfire. The area was out of earshot from where we lived but people closer to the event had complained about the noise. During the course of the evening the attending cretins required more wood for the fire so some bright spark decided that our fence would make good firewood. As it was later revealed about 20 young dickheads quietly removed the timber panels and some posts from our front fence and carried them half a kilometre down the beach to the party whereupon they threw them on the bonfire. Quite a feat to do silently and to carry them that distance as they were quite large and heavy panels. It was quite common knowledge that there were a few malcontents living on the west coast and if anything was untoward, like pinching flags as well, then this group of mentally challenged individuals were probably involved in some way.

It was not long before the sergeant had them rounded up and an "intervention" was arranged whereby, to avoid prosecution, those involved were required to attend some counselling sessions, community meetings to correct their attitude and behaviour, and some hours of community work. To some degree it must have worked because Strahan never had any more serious vandalism and of course those that committed this idiotic act are now reasonable adults. One of the young chaps was assigned to me to work for fifty hours at Ormiston House and he turned out to be quite a reasonable young chap in the end. The insurance claim was $11,000 and we got a new front fence and I used the old timbers for craft wood, so the end result was quite acceptable, although inconvenient.

Wasps and bees

We were very fortunate to have an excellent beekeeper in Strahan. His honey was, and still is, second to none. The bees collect their nectar from the wild-flowers and trees in the area producing a wonderful bush honey as well as a brilliant leatherwood. In addition, our local beekeeper was available if there were any bee swarms in the area. One day the nurse at the medical centre next to Ormiston House phoned us to say a huge bee swarm was heading our way. The housekeeper noticed that there were a few bees in one of the rooms; the swarm had settled into one of our chimneys and so we called our local beekeeper. The chimney was capped off as we had decommissioned the active fireplaces and the bees had found an entrance through a gap in the mortar between the bricks. The beekeeper said there was no way he could get access to the swarm to retrieve the queen, so our only option was to wait and hope the swarm moved on or use insecticide to kill the bees in the chimney. As we already had bookings for the room during that week, I decided to let some bombs off in the fireplace to kill the swarm. At great personal risk I entered the room with a quantity of bees flying around and placed one of the bombs in the fireplace. Luckily most of the bees in the room had migrated to the window. I pressed the button on the bomb, the insecticide released, and I made a hasty exit from the room. We waited about an hour and then I entered the bedroom. My god what a mess. The floor of the room was coated in dead bees and what was worse was that they must have had a lot of honey on them and that had mixed with the soot in the old chimney so that the carpet was covered in a black sticky mess of coagulated corpses. To make matters worse there were still live bees flying around so I closed the door, got another bomb and then edged the door open again and activated the bomb. Another hour later and all was quiet. I entered the room again trying not to tread on too many dead bees. When I did, I left a black blotch on the carpet. In the fireplace was a huge mound of dead bees and would you believe there was still buzzing up in the chimney; the swarm must have been massive. Once again, I retreated, returned with another bomb and placed it directly in the fireplace on top of the mound of dead bees and let it off and made a quick exit. After another hour or so I edged open the door and all was quiet. There were thousands and thousands of these poor dead bees everywhere. I felt terrible about the carnage but what else could we do?

Of course, we were in Strahan and no carpet cleaners available. We called a few up but we would have to wait for a week or two before they could get down the west coast. I spent the rest of that day and the next scooping up dead bees and then cleaning the carpet by hand. Surprisingly the honey and the soot came clean very easily with warm soapy water and some elbow grease. We dried the carpet off with heaters and fans and we were ready for guests within 24 hours. Just another day in the hospitality industry.

Wasps were an even worse pest as the emerging queens would often nest in crevices and in the roof cavity. They would then make their way down through the cavity in the outer brickwork and into the rooms through the ventilation grids. This only happened just as summer started but of course the guests would panic and one of us would have to calm the guest down and either shoo the wasp out of the room or kill the bastard in some way. Of course, the guests would usually be cooperative – not! At times you could spray them (the wasp not the guest…..although the thought often crossed my mind; I actually felt sorry for the poor bloody wasp), but not with the guest in the room as the room would have to be ventilated so opening the window was one option but also allowed other insects to come in. At times I would suggest they go into the bar for a short while; a passive suggestion as, under my breath, I would in fact be saying "just fuck off for a few minutes for Christ's sake and stop screaming like a raving banshee."

At one stage we had so many European wasps, those yellow and black bastards, that there had to be a nest close by. Alongside our property was a vacant block and our garden was 1.4 acres so a bit of territory to cover. I found the nest in our compost heap. Easy to find during the day but not recommended to go too close. Time for Mr Google. I did some online research and purchased some 'Baygon' powder. The plan was to wait until after sunset and then spray the powder around the entrance to the nest. The wasps would collect the powder on their bodies as they came and went eventually killing the nest and occupants. That was the theory, but I got a bit excited and thought I would give it a go during the day. Bad move. The buggars went berserk and I hastily retreated to the house until they settled down. I gave the entrance a good dose during the evening and stood at a safe distance the next day to observe the comings and goings. Life seemed normal on the first day but very restricted the following day, so I gave the nest another dose that evening. Within two days the nest was totally quiet, so I proceeded to investigate the compost heap. I expected the nest to be within the compost, but it was actually under the ground beneath the compost and was several metres in diameter in a rough shaped area. This was the first time I had seen a wasp nest and it was irregular in shape and covered with a paper like wrap around and full of a labyrinth of tunnels and hexagonal chambers. There were dead wasps everywhere thank goodness and after that episode we had reduced incidents with the little bastards. No doubt about it; we were surrounded by pests inside the house and outside as well.

Wildlife

Blue tongue lizards are great for the garden. They are also great for showing guests especially when they stick their tongue out and hiss. As well as eating all manner of garden pests such as slugs, snails and grasshoppers they also love strawberries as I found out to the detriment of the strawberry patch. I knew something or someone was getting into them as there were half eaten and masticated fruit laying around. My nightlife hidden camera caught the culprit who I named Jaws for obvious reasons. The UK guests, in particular, loved it when I would pick up the lizards and bring them into the house and show them the little critters. Some were quite large and whilst some houseguests reeled in horror most were totally fascinated.

We had some regular eastern green rosellas as seasonal visitors and over a few years we had tamed a small group of them so that they would settle on our hands and eat birdseed. The trick was not to let the seed run out as they would bite your fingers when the seed ran out. We had a few houseguests who were brave enough to join us and once again it was the UK visitors that enjoyed them the most....in fact many visitors from the UK were avid birdwatchers and our garden was full of a variety of Tasmanian birds.

No more Christmas music thanks

Christmas was a wonderful time in the house, made even more wonderful by the fact that we closed the house for five days each year so we could enjoy Christmas with family and friends without constant interruptions and whinging house guests. I say whinging because during Christmas time many businesses would either be closed like us or, as some of the eateries in town did, they would rotate their opening times so as to give staff some time off with families and at the same time ensure there were at least one or two eateries open at any given time. So over Christmas whether we opened or not it was an ample opportunity for visitors to the town to complain about services and attractions that were not open all day every day. Given that from Boxing Day onwards the town would be totally full for the best part of three months it was an opportunity over Christmas when the town was running at about 40% occupancy to give staff and owners some time to themselves and brace for the onslaught. We did open a couple of Christmas seasons during the first few years. The first time we did it the house guests were charming, non-invasive and required little input from us save breakfast and dinner, which they were happy to spend with us in a long table style Christmas fare. When we opened the following Christmas, the guests were the total opposite. Demanding, complaining, high maintenance and a total pain in the arse from the moment they arrived until they left. That was the last Christmas we opened for those five days. It was also made the more difficult with Carolyn's birthday on the 23rd December and I was also the town Santa and had around seven appearances and parade around town up to and including Christmas Eve. Trying to extricate ourselves from the business and the houseguests to attend to personal and community celebrations and duties was almost impossible. The simplest solution was to close even though the cessation of revenue was painful the exercise was good for the soul and gave us much needed preparation time for the forthcoming busy season. During the time we were in Strahan the community produced a Men in Strahan calendar. You guessed it, I was Mr December resplendent as Santa missing most of my apparel and laying on a chaise lounge. The photo crew were a couple of local ladies and the photograph took ages to take. Apparently, the props had to positioned correctly and they seemed most interested in Santa's sack. My first job as Santa arose after the previous Santa got pissed on the job and started throwing the presents from the gift tree at the kids instead of passing them. He got the sack, pardon the pun, and I was asked. For the first few years I used to get dressed at the fire station into my suit and had to wrap a blanket around me under the suit to give me some bulk. In the last few years no padding was required.

One problem we did have was that the town Christmas parade was on the 23rd December at around 6.30pm; the same day as Carolyn's birthday. That day was always a big one as I and friends would organise a variety of surprises for Carolyn, such as helicopter or boat trips. Of course, there was much sparkling wine and other drinks, the customary prawns and Tassie lobsters, frequently it was on a friend's large catamaran so there would be twenty or thirty of us chugging up and down the harbour in various stages of merriment. When the party was at its peak, I would have to get changed into my Santa suit and I would get dropped off at one of the jetties and the fire truck would pick me up. Sometimes I was a bit pissed. Luckily all I had to do was sit in the leading fire truck and wave and at the end of the parade give out some presents to the kids. One time I fell asleep much to the amusement of everyone. Another time I had my window down and one of the local youngsters stuck a fire hose through the window and soaked myself and the driver as well as the complete inside of the cab including the radio; the little shit.

Wine experts

My knowledge of wines, spirits and cocktails was reasonably good when we bought Ormiston House and, fairly rapidly, we developed an extensive cellar and wine list. The bar was set up well and I must admit I enjoyed dispensing the beverages as well as the interaction with our guests. Of course, some were painful but mostly quite genuine and interesting people. I went to great lengths to ensure the wine list was both entertaining and informative with quotations as well as detailed notes on each wine. I made it my business to know each of our wines intimately and with the help of our suppliers I was able to recommend most of our wines by personal experience. Our suppliers would regularly have tastings and when the wine reps called in, we would ensure any new offerings were tasted and ensure that our menu and wines would complement each other.

On many occasions the guests, both dinner or house, would seek my recommendations and usually all went well. The only instances I recall that did not go well were when the guest tried to emphasise his expertise in viticulture. There were some guests who were indeed knowledgeable and when there was no 'bullshit' we would have a most interesting conversation. However, when the guest waffled on with complete nonsense, I was compelled to keep quiet even though I would have loved to have shot them down. After all, above all else, why should I enlighten or criticise him (I can only recall males pontificating) when they are waxing lyrical about the more expensive wines on the list and if I let them have their way without contradiction I would be making a more than reasonable profit. Criticise and they get the shits and we will all have an unpleasant evening. Better to let them rave on in blissful ignorance and thank them when they hand over their credit card.

Even better when you agree with them and they leave you with a tip.

I recall a group of American travel agents one evening and the tour guide from Tourism Tasmania said give them a drink, whatever they want. One large lady, Texas I think, said in a loud voice what can I have? I looked at the tour guide and he just shrugged and so I said what would you like. She looked at our top shelf and said, "I'll have a Johnnie Walker Blue with coke." The tour guide nearly choked on his glass of chardonnay. He said, "how much did that just cost me." I said "$55.00". "Fuck me," he said. I was more appalled at the fact that someone would be idiotic enough to drink a premium scotch whisky with coke. I mean what is the fucking point; you can have a standard scotch and you would not taste the difference. Some people must have their taste buds in their arse.

Great grandfather in the cricket painting

There were two prints we acquired solely for the purpose of retaining when we inevitably sold Ormiston House. One of the limited-edition prints we had hanging in the hallway was the Lords cricket match of 1886 by I F Weedon which has cameos of the individual players surrounding the field painting. One of our houseguests was looking at it and then exclaimed that his great grandfather was one of the English players.

Alongside this print was another of a famous painting with a mysterious past, that of the famous rugby match played at Bradford in 1893 by William Barnes Woollen sometimes referred to as the War of the Roses between Lancashire and Yorkshire. If anyone is interested, I recommend they do some research as the story is quite interesting.

Berengaria and Lusitania

We deliberately chose wall art that would reflect the style of paintings that F O Henry would have had originally in the house, and that which would be interesting for the house guests as well. It would have been nice to be able to afford the original oil paintings, but we had enough trouble with our budget as it was.

On our way to Tasmania we stopped in Wangaratta for the night and saw an early 20th century etching of an ocean liner. The inscription was of the Berengaria departing Southampton. It was old and we decided it would look the part in the soon to be restored bar and lounge at Ormiston House. It turned out that although the drawing was an original it was in fact a copy of an image used by Cunard as a postcard and around the same time appeared as a cigarette card with WD & HO Wills. In any case the drawing was superb and still adorns behind the bar at the house.

Not too long after we opened, I did some research into the Berengaria and found out it was previously a German liner and after WW1 it was seconded to Cunard in compensation for sinking the Lusitania. I had a book on the Lusitania and whilst reading it I noticed a building on the Manhattan waterfront as the Lusitania was docking in New York. I mention that as both myself and our guests were often commenting on two prints of sailing ships in a harbour during the 1860s. Magnificent paintings but the location was debateable. It was the photo of the Lusitania that showed me that the building on the waterfront, and also in the paintings was Castle Clinton as it was in the 19th century and today pretty much of a ruin and bearing no resemblance to the building in both the photo image and the paintings. The city in the background was indeed New York during the mid-nineteenth century.

The Piano and the lunatic harmonium player

One day there was a knock on the front door. Not unusual in any respect as we would regularly get people looking for a sticky beak inside the house; whereby I would politely tell them we did not do tours. This chap in particular was a little different and asked if we had an antique piano or organ. He said he liked to play the older instruments and he recorded them. I asked what music he played, and he said mainly his own compositions. The house was quiet, no guests around so I told him the piano was out of tune, but the harmonium was in good condition. I showed him into one of the dining rooms and he set himself up and started to play. I did not hang around as I had jobs to do but I did hear a bit of unrecognisable notes as I walked away.

About half an hour later I went back to see how he was going and listened to the notes he was playing. I have a musical background from learning piano accordion and classical music when I was a youngster. I quickly assessed that this chap was not really playing anything other than a mish mash of notes. Whether he regarded them as his own compositions or not it became exceedingly obvious that this chap was an absolute fucking nutter. He was posturing over the keyboard like some lunatic virtuoso playing Rachmaninoff but essentially it was total crap. What should I do? I decided to leave him for a while but walked in the near vicinity. His eyes were closed, and he was totally off with the fairies and there was the god-awful cacophony of mixed up notes.

After another hour I had to tap him on the shoulder and tell him we had house guests arriving soon. He thanked me, turned his recorder off and then asked me if I knew of any other places that had a piano or organ. For a bit of a laugh I sent him to another property who I knew would not be as cordial as myself. I saw the chap still wandering around town a couple of days later and had to laugh when around the same time I bumped into the property owner where I had sent him previously. He told me about this loopy guy who called in to play his piano. He said, "I don't have a piano mate, piss off."

Drivers on the road

Now I know when you are on holiday you are not in a hurry so most of the time when you are driving around you take in the sights and not rushing around. If the speed limit is 100km and scenery is good you cruise a bit slower. However, if the scenery is great and the roads have double lines and lots of corners and hills and you are toddling along at a modest pace then odds are someone is going to come up in your rear vision mirror. Chances are that he, or she, is behind you now because they are travelling faster than you. It could also be that the driver is local or is on business and unlike you does not have the time to be cruising along at half the speed limit.

In many cases they will be familiar with the road and champing at the bit to get past you. Some roads have regular passing areas where there is a left lane for slow vehicles to move into. Many mountain and country roads do not however they do have small gravel 'pull over' areas that you can move into and allow people who do not have as much time on their hands as you do to pass. "So why the fuck don't you quickly move over and let them pass?" This goes double for motor homes and caravans. In Tasmania we have many country roads that have double lines for many kilometres and few opportunities to overtake safely. Some drivers do keep an eye on their rear and if they see cars moving up quickly behind them, they move over at the first opportunity and let them pass.

Unfortunately, more often locals, and other drivers without the luxury of time, get stuck for kilometres behind inconsiderate arseholes who are either oblivious to other drivers or who deliberately refuse to render some courtesy to the ever-increasing number of vehicles building up in their rear vision mirror. At times I know it would seem that the car directly behind is tailgating, but more often they have to stay close as the opportunity to safely overtake will be brief. Would it not be much simpler to pull over into one of the cleared areas and wave them through? There are many trucks on the roads these days, but truckies will more than often allow you to pass them safely at the first opportunity on narrow winding roads by pulling over to the left and waving you on.

On one occasion I came around a corner in a 100km zone and a car was stopped in the middle of the road across the centre double lines with the windows down and people inside taking photos. Yes, they did get a mouthful from me after I screeched to a halt. They were lucky I was not a fast-moving heavy vehicle. Message to tourists, caravans and motorhomes - pull over on narrow country roads and let the faster traffic through and don't be a discourteous arsehole.

On that subject I have often wondered how we could filter out the "arseholes on holiday." Among my musings was the concept of an Arsehole Squad. There are sniffer dogs for drugs, plants and explosives: why not arseholes? Dogs are also very good judges of human character and if someone is decidedly unpleasant dogs can react accordingly or avoid the person in question. I thought about a sniffer dog to weed out the unpleasant individuals at airports and ferries. Most would be males I suspect and in company with their wives who would be more than well aware of their partner's shortcomings. I envisage an encounter something like this. The dog would growl at the suspected "arsehole". The officer would approach the individual and say. "Excuse me sir, this dog has detected the possibility of you being an arsehole."

To which the individual would reply. "Fuck off mate, you're talking shit."

The officer would turn to his travelling companion. "Excuse me ma'am, this dog suspects your companion of being an arsehole?"

To which the lady replies, "Oh yes he is, a right arsehole."

The officer then replies, "Thank you Ma'am, your companion will be returning on the next flight, but we would like to offer you a voucher for a hire car during your visit, and some dinner and tour vouchers. Thank you for your co-operation."

The woman gratefully accepts the vouchers and proceeds to have a completely enjoyable holiday without her arsehole of a husband.

I think it could work.

Diets

Please, if you have any dietary requirements or allergies while on holidays let the place you are staying, or the eatery you have booked into, know instead of telling them when you are sitting down looking at the menu. Give us a bit of fucking notice and we will be more than happy to assist with your special needs and your imaginary ones as well. Unlike one of our guests who informed us at the table that the husband has a sever reaction to sesame seeds. Great. All of our bread rolls at that time had sesame seeds on them. Then to be told he is so sensitive that even if food in the kitchen comes into contact where sesame seeds or sesame oil have been, he could go into anaphylactic shock. For fuck's sake if an allergy is so severe why not tell us before your arrival, are you terminally stupid. Luckily, we were not that busy that particular evening, so the chef washed down all the benches, utensils and pans again before his food was prepared just in case any seeds had contaminated the surfaces.

The guest survived his stay with us, and his wife said that they would definitely be back as we looked after them so well. After they departed, we put them on our 'black list'. Carolyn, myself and the chef were totally paranoid the whole time they were with us in case the prick carked on us. Dead guests are not good for business, and most inconvenient

Chapter Thirty-four

'rats, banks and paid companions'

Rats

I really hate to admit this one, but it is a fact of life that in any house, no matter how hard you try, these little fuckers can find their way in. It bears no reflection on the standard of cleanliness or hygiene in the property. The incidents we had were isolated and infrequent but when they occurred we were horrified and much of the time in panic should a guest see one before we could take remedial action.

The first incident I recall was when I noticed that one of the apples was missing from the bowl of fruit at reception. A little later during service I found a partly chewed apple in one of the fireplace hearths. I called the alert and a thorough inspection was made by us all. We really were shitting ourselves that there was a rat or rats loose in the house. The inspection showed no further evidence however that night we put some rat traps out and removed the fresh fruit from reception. The next morning the traps had not been touched. Damn. We knew the rats must still be around. I called the pest control and of course no-one could make it down, but he would send down some glue boards which he said were very effective, but I would have to despatch the little blighter once it was caught. One more night of traps but no rats and then the glue boards arrive the next day.

That night we put glue boards along the main passageways. In the morning up bright and early before the guests and one of the glue boards is missing but where can it be? We pick up the untouched boards and inspect the ground floor areas hoping that the damn rat has not squeezed under the doors into any of the rooms attached to a glue board. I open the door leading up to the attic where we have a history room and there sitting on the stairs is a glue board and the tail of a rat. The rat had got his tail caught on the glue board, squeezed under the door to the attic with the glue board attached to his tail and then chewed his own tail off to escape from the board. It was a big fat tail and I guessed we had a big fat rat with a missing tail. There was a faint blood trail that led up to the attic and to one of the roof space doors. That day I set up some glue boards in the attic and sealed up the gap under the roof space door. The rat was trapped in the roof space.

The next morning, I waited until after breakfast when the house guests had departed and opened up the roof space door and there was the biggest, meanest, rat I have seen. It was hissing at me but was firmly attached to two glue boards and could not move around. His hair was course like on an old scrubbing brush and he had an angry, defiant look in his eyes. It was like something out of a horror movie. Where had this monster come from? Hollywood was my guess; straight out of a Boris Karloff movie. I grabbed a box and slipped him into it almost afraid he would reach up and snap at me with his enormous yellow stained front teeth. Anyway, he got a wack on the head and straight to the tip with the rubbish that morning. Upon my return I was greeted enthusiastically by Carolyn and the staff as the undisputed white hunter of feral beasties.

Of course, rats were not a common occurrence but, on another occasion, we did see one running down the passageway one day and during the subsequent chase it ended up under the pedals of the harmonium. I guessed that the only way out would be the way it went in, so I called for help while I got some glue boards. I then placed the glue boards around the pedals so that the rat had to cross a glue board to get away. Sure enough, after about 30 mins as I was waiting behind the door, I saw it venture out and wham, it got caught. Once again quickly despatched and congratulations again to my intrepid hunting skills.

Mice can also be a problem but easier to catch and to eradicate. We knew there was one around as we would find a little dropping every now and then behind the bar counter. After a few days the little buggar had still eluded us and despite the traps and glue boards we had not caught it. One evening whilst we were serving dinners a couple were seated next to a window. While I was taking their order, a mouse walked along the window ledge. I thought the lady seated to my right was going to scream but she observed it with some amusement as it ran down the curtain. I stood there in absolute silence. I had a look of horror on my face as it ran across the hallway and into the bar. She said, "go get it", I said "OK." Great, it was out of the dining room and with no one in the bar I was free to go into hunting mode. I put some cheese on the counter behind the bar and surrounded it with 4 glue boards so to get to the cheese the mouse had to cross a glue board. Within 30 minutes the mouse was looking at the cheese and 5 mins later stuck and disposed of. The guests were watching me from their table and then gave me the thumbs up. It just goes to show that the same circumstances with different guests could have delivered a terrible outcome. That was the only 'rodent to guest' up close and personal incident we had. I think.

Paid Companions

Operating a B&B brings one into contact with many walks of life. Unlike cheap hotels and motels in seedy areas we rarely see the dark side of the street, so to speak. We have a friend who bought a sizeable motel some years ago in a coastal town and among his repeat guests were some ladies of the night. They required a room, preferable towards the back and close to a side entrance away from the main reception. They would stay for few days and have a regular clientele visiting and then they would move on to another location. They kept to themselves, left the room in a clean and tidy condition, did their own laundry and in general terms were considered to be a good guest. They paid cash, what a surprise, and over time they stopped coming and no doubt this was part of their *'modus operandi'* to move around.

We never experienced a 'professional' guest of that genre however I do recall two guests, both male who had a partner with them who I could only describe as a person of interest. Both males were, I guess, elderly and in their late 60s. The first guest in question was during the early days and was visiting in one of those years when we were open for guests during Christmas.

From memory it was this Christmas that influenced our decision to close for a few days and have some family time in future years. The gentleman was, as I said, in his late 60s and his companion was an exceptionally good-looking young man in his mid-twenties. Tall, blond and with a good physique he was charming and affable. The older man, on the other hand, was balding, obese and rude. The younger man did the check in, the older man paid when he checked out. They stayed in a room with an antique four poster bed which for us was not a problem as we were a 'gay friendly' establishment and displayed a rainbow sign at the reception area. During their visit the older man was repeatedly rude and almost abusive to the younger man; to the point where I was close to intervention as this was making the other guests uncomfortable. This interaction between guests was in the bar area and the dining room. Made the more uncomfortable as many of the attractions and eateries were

211

closed on Christmas Day and the guests were inhouse most of the time. At one point during Christmas Day the older man ordered the younger man back to their room, mainly I believe, because the other guests were conversing with him and ignoring the older. The younger man complied, smiled to everyone and with some degree of embarrassment left. We did not see the younger man again until they left on Boxing Day, much to our, and the other guests' relief. To state the obvious, in my opinion, he was a paid companion. One of the most pleasurable aspects of owning and operating a bed and breakfast establishment is that there is always going to be a higher level of interaction with the guests. In most cases this will be a positive experience for guests and hosts but at times it does expose each of us to the foibles of the other.

The other visitor experience was much more interesting and pleasant. We had a direct booking from the UK for a couple in February obviously escaping the cold UK winter. The lady did the 'check in' with an address in Scotland and was significantly younger than her male companion. Their surnames were different but hey, so are mine and Carolyn's. He was Scottish and spoke with a stout brogue and she had an educated British accent, decidedly London I thought.

They adjourned to their room and at that time we did not do evening meals, so they visited a local restaurant and we did not see them until breakfast. Prior to check out the lady was looking at the pictures on our dining room walls where they had breakfast. The gentleman had returned to their room. I started a conversation with this very attractive and polished lady, and she spoke of their journey around Tasmania and of their visit to a luxury yacht whilst in Hobart. I have an interest in ships and boats and I enquired if it was the visiting mega yacht which was on the news the previous evening. She said it was and that the owner of the yacht was a client of the Gentlemen's Club in London where she worked. Now me being the slow minded individual I can be sometimes envisaged stuffy old rooms resplendent in wall to wall bookshelves, chesterfield lounges and cigar puffing bureaucrats. Then she said quite openly that the club was having the 'rooms' renovated over winter and "Jock" had invited her on a holiday. She also mentioned the owner of the vessel and quite openly again some of the high-profile patrons of the club in which she worked. I then realised what kind of establishment she worked in and, given the names of the patrons, that she was a very high-class employee of the same. Just when the conversation was starting to get interesting "Jock" came back into the dining room and gave me a very gruff look and saying to the lady that they needed to go.

It was interesting that she carried/wheeled the bags out to the car while he paid the bill. Usually it is the other way around or the man does both. She smiled and gave me a wink as she passed reception while he had a look like thunder and abruptly walked out after paying without bidding farewell as most guests do. I must confess to Googling the male client and not without surprise to see he was a significant landholder in Scotland... The owner of the mega yacht was an extremely high-profile billionaire......say no more!

Bastards!

Sometime toward the end of our first year of operation in late 1996 we had a visit from a person we thought we recognised. As they came to the front door I said to Carolyn, they are our neighbours from Brisbane. They were on a Tasmanian holiday and thought they would just pop in and say hello. During the conversation over a cup of coffee in the bar the subject of the new owners of our Brisbane house was raised. This was of interest to us as the bank we were with had insisted that we sell the house within twelve months of acquiring the bridging finance. We objected due to the state of the housing market and that we had no real offers to consider. We had the house on the market for $340,000 which at the time was a reasonable price for the property. We contacted the real estate agent and he told us that he had only received one offer for $260,000. We said we would get back to him.

In hindsight we should have contacted a solicitor to act on our behalf and stall the sale until the market improved. Instead we were stupid enough to tell the bank that our only offer was $260,000 and that we wanted to wait until the market improved. Carolyn owned the house outright, but it was mortgaged as security against the bridging finance. At that stage we were making the required interest only payments within our budget. The bank insisted that we take the 'offer' or they would call in the loan. We capitulated and told the real estate agent to accept the offer. In retrospect and now with more experience with banks we should have called in a solicitor and financial advisor.

Now we move forward to six months after the house sold when we are talking to our old neighbour. We ask him who are the new neighbours. He tells us that he is a recently retired bank manager from the ******* bank. What a coincidence that is our bank as well. Bastards. Et tu, Brute. Isn't it great to have financial partners that have your best interests at 'heart'. Yes, we changed banks and will never deal with that bastard bank again

Chapter Thirty-five

'a couple of memorable B&Bs'

I, like many of you, have spent some time as a guest in other establishments. I recall a trip I did to the UK some years ago. There are some absolute gems that will remain in my memory forever. The most memorable experience was when I was driving around the coastline from London, north to John O'Groats, across the top, down the west coast of Scotland and then into Wales. It was late afternoon and I was looking for somewhere to stay. Little did I know that I had cousins living at Aberystwyth otherwise I would have stopped there. I drove southward stopping at a place called Brynhoffnant and looked in my directory of B & Bs and guesthouses. There was a farm guesthouse close by called 'Morfa Isaf' so I called and the lady told me how to get there. I remember driving down extremely narrow laneways and luckily did not meet another car coming the other way as there was no way two cars could pass. A wonderful lady called Beryl greeted me and showed me to my room. She suggested I take a walk through the farm and give her Labrador a walk at the same time. I was travelling by myself and was glad to stretch my legs amid this 16th century farmhouse land. The dog obviously knew the way and I got the impression that I was not the first person he had shown around. I stopped at a WW2 communications station on the cliff top. The dog decided he was bored with my company, so he went back and left me to wander along the cliff top. I was gone about an hour and when I got back Beryl had the fire going and some lovely tucker and a hot drink. We sat by the fire and chatted and then she reached for her guitar and sung me some welsh ballads. This went on for some time I guess and with the sun setting around 10pm darkness was my queue to turn in. I had a four-poster bed in an en-suited room and the whole experience was pleasantly surreal. What was amazing was the genuine warmth and hospitality of the owner.

Another great place was the Forest Lodge Hotel at Edwinstowe a little earlier in my travels. I had just visited my cousins at Newark–on–Trent and was keen to get some miles up that day. I was sitting at the bar talking to John and Carol, the hosts, and this old guy comes up to me and says, "you by yourself lad." In a thick north country accent. "Come and sit with me and I'll tell ya all about pit." Fred as it turned out was a regular at the pub and called in every night for a couple of pints. He was easily in his eighties I reckon, dressed in a tweed suit, tweed hat and I guess a tweed overcoat. His conversation was only interrupted by a swig of beer and a puff on his pipe. Fred had worked in the coalmines all his life and right from when he was a boy he looked after the pit ponies. Now he must have talked non-stop for a couple of hours during which time I had my dinner at his table and a couple of beers myself. John, the host, told me later that Fred does this every night. He spots someone sitting by themselves, as I was, and warmly ushers them to his table.

I must say I enjoyed the chat although I did very little talking. But what it did do was make my visit there so memorable. Fred was indeed a bit of a treasure although I doubt if he is still around. John and Carol have since moved on also but both Forest Lodge and Morfa Isaf are two places

I am going back to. I've said it before, and I'll say it again this is the true hospitality experience that makes it a pleasure to be in the industry and makes it great for visitors.

Chapter Thirty-six

'are you really cut out for this job'

There are a number of ways to get into the B & B industry.

1. Purchase an existing B & B property
2. Lease an existing B & B business
3. Manage a B & B
4. Build and open a brand new B & B
5. Purchase a building and convert into a B & B
6. Convert your existing home into a B & B

Regardless of any of the above there is the issue of motive. What has motivated you to get into this industry? Are you as thoroughly prepared as you should be for what will be a complete transition from anything else you may have done? This is regardless of whether you have had previous hospitality experience or not. Most certainly working in hospitality in a previous life would be an advantage as suddenly working with the public in an up close, personal face to face situation can be a daunting experience for the uninitiated. Quite frankly it does not get more up close and personal than in a B & B.

For many couples owning and operating a B & B is something they have felt they would like to do at some stage and for those couples I would say go ahead but make sure you do your homework first.

B & B owners and other small accommodation providers bring a huge range of skills to the tourism and hospitality industry. The hosts in this industry, particularly B & Bs, in many cases have professional backgrounds in a range of disciplines. In addition, they are usually 45 years plus in age and will also have a scope of lifetime experiences to back that up. Owning and operating a B & B is a lifestyle decision but not a lifetime occupation. Invariably the lifespan of owning and operating a B & B will usually occupy on average about 5 to 10 years. Some leave early for a variety of reasons while others like ourselves will stay on for longer. Some may find it rewarding during retirement and a way of meeting new and interesting people.

One question that springs to mind is that of personality. If you enjoy meeting people, and you have a wide circle of friends, this is a good start. If you do not have a quick temper, and you deal with crisis in a calm and controlled manner, then this will be an advantage. You will need a good sense of humour and above all have a likeable personality.

If on the other hand you do not enjoy meeting people you have never met before, have a quick temper, no sense of humour and are not good in a crisis then this may not be the vocation for you.

Another important aspect is that with a B&B you will be operating a business. As with other businesses there are regulations and standards that have to be adhered to regardless of whether your B & B will be a casual affair with one or two rooms and taking in guests when it is convenient to a full on business with reservation systems, staff and even perhaps an in-house restaurant.

This brings us to another important issue, that of finance. You may be purchasing or leasing but be aware of how much you can afford and how much you will rely upon the revenue from selling rooms to repay loan commitments. In this day and age, you will get little cooperation and no assistance from banks and finance companies if you over-extend yourselves and cannot meet your financial obligations. You will not only risk losing your business but your home as well. No matter how much you want to own or operate a B & B in the next phase of your life do not borrow extensively to get there and risk losing it all. There is no real formula regarding finance as each situation must be based on its own merits. There is a distinct advantage for a small B & B, say up to 5 rooms, and that is for one of the owners to stay in their job during the establishment phase. Better to employ a housekeeper and keep one job than rely on the business to yield the equivalent of two incomes with both of you doing all the work.

The ideal solution is to be totally cashed up, own the business outright from the beginning and have cash in reserves for working capital. This will deliver peace of mind especially if it takes a while to build up customer patronage. This also gives you the flexibility of choosing when to accept guests and when to take a well-earned break without the worry of meeting financial commitments during a closed period.

This brings us to the other important aspect of location. Just as location is important in the acquisition of any real estate, so too it is important when choosing or building a B & B. If the objective is to be as busy as possible then choose a popular tourism destination which also has commercial visitation as well. Tourism alone can be seasonal and commercial business will be quiet during holiday times and in the case of an industry closing or leaving the area. A combination of the two is best. If lifestyle is the priority the location is not so important in terms of visitation to the area and subsequent revenue. Bear in mind that even in a lifestyle business there are operating costs that will need to be met.

Purchasing an existing B & B, with hindsight, would be my first choice. Whilst we restored and then opened a new business, I would not go down that path again. We purchased and restored in 1995. A lot has changed with building regulations and industry requirements since then and together with renovation and restoration costs I would choose an existing business as a preference.

I see many advantages with purchasing an existing business in terms of an established market presence. This should not be understated and can be the difference with moving into immediate profit or positive cash flow as opposed to a long period of time establishing patronage that provides adequate revenue.

You would need to examine an existing business carefully and do not be afraid to employ someone who is experienced in this industry to assist you in making an informed decision. This would not just be a real estate agent or even an accountant although you would need to consult with your financial advisors. The point I am trying to make is that if you are going to buy a business talk to someone who knows that type of business. An accountant will tell you if the books and accounts are being managed properly and if the business on paper is viable. He will also be able to advise you on what finance is recommended based on the ability of the business to repay. Remember if you are going to borrow that there always needs to be enough left over to live on and also what I call a 'buggar factor'. You will need to be assured that there is a safety net in the equation in case something 'buggars up'. That amount would be left over at the end of the day in case something goes wrong or you get an unexpected expense. Believe me those situations crop up more often than you would think.

Talking to someone, who has had hands on experience in operating a B&B, in my view, is as essential as talking to an accountant. There are people, like me, who have spent many years in tourism and hospitality who are able to visit the business and immediately recognise both problems and attributes. I do not say this to solicit business but please discuss your project with someone in the industry. Do not hold back on the expense of employing someone who could save you a lot of money and heartache in what may be one of the most important purchases of your life. Purchasing on the basis of 'pure emotion' can have devastating results.

Some of us who have done extensive restoration on old and heritage buildings can provide essential advice on how these buildings need to be looked after when running a B & B. In my view the perfect couple to own and operate a B & B will have one of them that loves to cook and the other a good handyman or tradesperson. Other skills are important as well and these days at least one of the 'partnership' needs to have computer knowledge and also aspects of social media. If one or both like gardening and cooking then they will have a lot of fun at the same time.

Leasing a B & B is probably the best option for anyone who does not have the capacity to purchase outright. It may also be a good platform to purchase further down the track if all parties are agreeable. The downside is that the building is not yours and you will be restricted in what you can do in terms of improvements. If the owner is a reasonable person and there is a benefit for them then there is no reason why the business can't be 'improved' and the property enhanced at the same time.

When leasing the trick is to sell while you still have an ongoing lease for a new purchaser. There is the risk of the lease not being renewed and if you end up staying until the lease runs out then you really have nothing to sell. Like many property transactions, if you have a reasonable landlord and you are a reasonable tenant there is every chance that both of you will work towards a mutual goal and understanding. If there are any doubts at the onset, then walk away. There will always be other businesses available so do not let your heart rule your head.

Ensure that when you enter into an agreement that there is adequate revenue in the business to meet commitments. Do the same as for purchasing and get someone to have a close look at the property and business who knows the industry. Using a good lawyer and accountant is essential once again. If you have previously owned or operated a B & B then you will understand what you are entering into and will be aware of any risks.

The existing profile in the marketplace and occupancy is just as important for a leased property as it is for one that you purchase. Building up the property's marketing profile would be an immediate task for any new owner/operator. Accreditation is becoming a necessity in tourism and hospitality businesses and offers advantages. The Tourism Council in Australia administer the scheme. Considering that you have only bought the business and are basically renting the building you will still have the majority of the costs even though you do not own the building.

Ensure that you and the owner of the building are aware of what your responsibilities are and ensure they are in the agreement. Busted hot water systems in a roof can be catastrophic and loss of business can ensue so make sure all bases are covered and each party is adequately insured against the unusual as well as the perceived inevitable. There are insurance companies that provide specific insurance packages for B & Bs.

These are by no means the only factors to look at and a purchaser would be well advised to seek assistance whether it is a lease or outright purchase.

Starting a B & B from scratch, in my view, can be a very expensive exercise. If all you want to do is have a couple of house guests at a time then your costs in providing a bed and breakfast establishment will be modest compared to renovating a heritage property or larger building such as an old school, church or any other significant change of use situation. Aside from the building works there will be compliance issues and then establishing a business in a very competitive marketplace.

To get a feel for hospitality and tourism you could, as a couple, take on the management of a small motel or B&B. This will give you an idea of whether you will both enjoy and have longevity in this industry. Believe me it won't take long to find that out. Some people may think they are cut out for this industry, but many

have found they are not and trying to leave an industry quickly after a significant investment can be an expensive exercise.

Chapter Thirty-seven

'be a team player and join in'

Over the years we have seen many tourism operators come and go. With both of us having experience with regional tourism boards, and both of us chairing those boards for many years, we have hands on experience dealing with other tourism operators, regional and state tourism organisations and other tourism related entities.

The biggest problem with towns and regional tourism groups is apathy. When times are good, they are all happy making money and don't feel the necessity to be overly pro-active. When times are not so good, they run around looking for someone else to blame why they are not making so much money when in most cases the fault lies within the individual businesses. There are some that make a lot of noise, like to have their opinions heard as they perk up at meetings and wax lyrical about the solutions to everyone's problems but never actually do anything tangible themselves. Sometimes they will get off their backsides but usually only when something will directly benefit their own business. When it comes to doing something for the benefit of the region, or the collective, they strangely go missing. They are too busy to do some of the work behind the scenes. In most cases there will be a few hard-working tourism operators who see the benefits of having a pro-active destination and they will be the ones who do most of the work; usually to the detriment of their own businesses. However, the slack arses who do all the talking and none of the work will be the first to criticise those that make the effort and accuse them of benefitting most from the marketing or activity in question.

My advice would be that if you are considering operating a tourism related business then be a participant, be a working board member and think of the big picture. Be a professional in the way you regard your business, your customers, your business associates and have respect for those that you deal with.

The most success the west coast of Tasmania had as a destination was in the late 1990s and early 2000s. Most of the tourism businesses were independently owned and were owner operated. The regional tourism group, when I was chair, had 69 paid up members and there was a hard-working board and executive made up of tourism operators who physically ran the organisation. We held and hosted tourism conferences, some of them with more attendance than statewide events. We held long table dinners in tandem with training organisations and TAFE and through dedicated participation the majority of the tourism operators went through a very profitable period. So why did that not continue?

One operator grew rapidly and bought out a number of smaller businesses in both accommodation and activity. Apathy set in amongst some of the operators who had it too good for too long thinking that they did not have to participate at such a high level. The larger operator started discounting to get more business at the disadvantage of the smaller operators which started a discount war. The online travel agent platforms such as Wotif, Booking.com, Expedia and the rest were positioning themselves into the transaction between customer and supplier causing further discounting and discontent among operators. Instead of a cooperative perspective within the destination it was now extremely internally competitive and every one's profit margins were falling. The management of Tourism Tasmania were closing the state wholesaler Tasmania's Temptations holidays right at a time when they should have been embracing the online environment. Instead they shrunk from some of the initiatives at a time when they and the state were at a distinctive advantage. The state had also recently closed down the other capital city tourism centres in the mainland capitals. Disillusioned operators started putting their properties on the market. The two major activity operators were in all out aggressive competition. Some

of the smaller activity operators either reduced hours or closed down.

In some ways a perfect storm and, regrettably, to the benefit of some of our regional neighbours who still had a cohesive group of tourism operators and management. In reality there were some real challenges but made worse because the local industry was not working as a team. During this time the west coast had, and still has, a council that never appreciated the tourism industry and the benefits it brought to the region. The west coast was historically a mining community since the 1880s and unfortunately some of the councillors and the community never saw the benefits of tourism until very recently. Consequently, the council has been very reluctant to fund tourism to the amount it should have done over the years and to some degree is paying the price now. Which, in itself, is sad because the west coast of Tasmania is a great tourism destination with wonderful products and wilderness environment.

Move ahead to today and now due to state government regulations we have a very unlevel playing field whereby the sharing economy products such as Airbnb and Uber are competing with those tourism operators that are subject to ever increasing costs in compliance as licensed tourism operators. The situation is fluid and will no doubt change over ensuing years. I don't think anyone expects politicians to be experts in any of its portfolios but nevertheless reliant on its advisors and senior bureaucrats to make the right decisions. In that regard whoever advised our state premier and government regarding Airbnb and Uber made some cardinal errors. The state government even went in opposition and away from the recommendations and advice of our own State Tourism Industry Council. The mess we are now in (2020) 'beggar's belief' with an out of control rental housing crisis which is of the state government's own making. I believe that at the time of writing some destinations around the world are in the process of reigning in Airbnb properties and providing more regulations. Not all, but most, Airbnb operators are in the business for entirely the wrong reasons. They are there for the sole purpose of getting as much bang for their buck out of a piece of real estate and Airbnb have made it so easy for them.

Today many accredited and bona fide tourism accommodation properties also list on Airbnb. The bona fide operators have all the correct insurances in place and you as a guest can be assured that if any incident occurs then the property has you covered. Accredited properties undergo regular inspections and assessments to ensure that you the guest, do indeed receive the level of service and quality that is advertised.

Suffice to say that anyone interested in providing short term holiday accommodation should do so for the right reasons and not just with a view to extracting as much money out of a property without making a tangible contribution to the local

economy. Most online platforms are based overseas and that is lost revenue for Australia.

Cooperative Marketing

One of the most effective and rewarding ways to market an accommodation business is to join a group of like-minded businesses. This can be by joining a formal marketing group or simply by working with other businesses in joint marketing. When we opened for business in 1995, we joined several small formal and informal groups. The most significant of these groups was Historic Houses of Tasmania; a group of notable historic properties offering hosted accommodation to what was then regarded as a high standard. When we opened Ormiston House, we raised the bar of hosted accommodation and other properties in Tasmania were quick to follow. Today there are many notable guesthouse style accommodation properties that offer exceptional quality throughout Australia and overseas.

We came into the market as the luxury end of hosted accommodation was cutting through and we quickly gained a reputation for our quality and level of service. We particularly enjoyed our membership of Historic Houses of Tasmania and the company of fellow hoteliers of the same ilk. Some, in our opinion, were a bit eccentric and odd but this all added to the flavour of the group in many ways. I did comment to Carolyn that as some of the members had been in the industry for some years that we should ensure we did not stay as long as they had already spent in hosted accommodation in case we became as eccentric and odd as some in the room. I say that with a degree of affection as the group was tremendously successful over a period of some years and each owner contributed to that success. One had me particularly puzzled when he showed me what had been assessed as the oldest bottle of Champagne in Australia. They had found it in the cellar when restoring the property. However, they did not have it on display, rarely told the guests about it and had boarded up the cellar where it had been found. "Why?" I asked, "this is a great feature and point of difference for your business." A shrug of the shoulders was the only reply as I recall.

Chapter Thirty-eight

'reviews – a love hate relationship'

There are cowboys in any industry, and they will always let the side down. Never stay in a place without reading recent reviews. Look at the last 10 reviews. Take out the very best and the very worst and then see what the other 8 reviews say. Taking a cross section of reviews will give you a general indication of whether the property is worth visiting. Today many OTA sites and others provide reviews. The first to do so was TripAdvisor and from a guest perspective extremely useful. One of the major problems with TripAdvisor is that there are two sets of rules. One for the guest and another for the property owner. Basically, the guest can say what they like about the property, but the property owner is censored heavily by how they can structure a reply. In the case of terminally stupid guests they can bad mouth a property with a load of horse shit and if the accommodation property rejects the complaint in its entirety then they will not have the reply posted.

Sites such as TripAdvisor have given the visitor their 5 minutes of fame over the internet to a worldwide audience. So much so that they can say whatever they like whether it be truthful and substantiated or not. In some examples a bad review can have a devastating effect on the business. At times justified, and in many cases not so. I recall a food critic in Australia many years ago who got so full of his own piss, importance and opinion that when he gave a restaurant a thorough rogering the restaurant had to close and in return he got sued by the proprietor.

There has been some legal action in relation to reviews so to this end there is a need to exercise caution when giving a property or restaurant a bad review. Make sure you are being factual and ensure that you provide some evidence to back up your claim especially if you are being aggressive or vitriol in your statements. It could be that you as a customer feel justified if the food, accommodation or service is appalling. If so why didn't you state your case at the time, confront the manager and either refuse to pay or return the food to the kitchen instead of paying your bill, saying nothing at the time and then tapping away on the keyboard like some pathological woodpecker after you have retreated to a safe haven. I can understand the reluctance of someone to be confrontational in public or to be afraid of potential physical retaliation however if you believe you are right then you should have nothing to fear especially if there are witnesses on your behalf.

We did have a few negative reviews and if they were of a reasonable nature, and justified we took them on board. One of them referred to a strange person who popped into the bar and asked if they required a drink. Obviously that strange person was me. What else is a barman supposed to do I ask?

The other I recall involved a lady who was not happy with her room. She stayed with us during what we call the off season. This was during the colder months in Tasmania and we had sold the room that night on a special discount of $99.00 including a continental breakfast. Normally this room in winter would have been selling for about $150.00. This review was exceptionally interesting considering that this guest was the first person in this room after it had been closed for six weeks for restoration work. We had a leak from a hot water system that had saturated one of the internal brick walls resulting in a lot of internal damage from the water. The result of that damage was a significant insurance claim whereby we had to close the room while we removed wallpaper in the bedroom and tiles in the adjacent en-suite. The plaster and brick walls had to be dried out by commercial equipment over a period of weeks.

During that time all fabrics in the room were removed and cleaned. The wallpaper was replaced by professional painters and decorators and all wood trim was re-painted while they were there. The wall tiles in the bathroom were replaced on two of the walls and the floor tiling was re-grouted. The carpets were also cleaned, fabrics replaced and the furniture polished. Essentially it was a new room albeit in period décor. This whole process, including allowing the room to air for a few days after all the work was done, took six weeks. This lady and her husband were the first guests. During her one-night stay there was no mention of any dissatisfaction and we bid them farewell after breakfast.

About a week later we got the message from TripAdvisor that there was a review just posted. I log on and I am 'absolutely aghast' at the shocking review about the poor standard of the room and how it was desperately in need of a refurbishment. I immediately did a reply through the TripAdvisor system only to receive a message from TripAdvisor that they would not post my reply. I was not offensive or aggressive in any of my remarks, but I firmly refuted her claims. I redrafted another reply and this too was rejected by TripAdvisor. By now I was 'fuck this' and 'fuck that' and 'fuck TripAdvisor' and then I thought well fuck you lot I will play your silly game. I then drafted another reply and commenced with the words "We are sorry" and continued to reply using apologetic phrases but at the same time explaining the lengths we go to, thus neutralising the complaint to some degree. The reply was then posted, and I would note that this was quite some years ago and very early in the TripAdvisor years for us.

In those years I did the replies and they were usually thanking them very much for their kind words. In fact, most of our trip advisor reviews from memory were quite positive and constructive. Back to this bad review. All our guests sign a registration card, so it was not difficult to identify this particular houseguest who at this time had only made two reviews, a bad one for us and good one for a property in the north west of Tasmania from memory. So, I wrote her the letter that TripAdvisor would not post for me pointing out that the room she found so deplorable had in fact just been open after a 'six-week' refurbishment. I was not offensive, but I was firm and that I found it unfathomable that she did not have the decency to complain in person if in fact the room was so bad. I recollect that most of the complaints, and there were few in that regard over the years, were made by people who had stayed at a discount rate and who probably would not have stayed with us at our regular prices. This was one of the reasons we resisted discounting most of the time ....one way to keep out the riff raff. I remain firmly convinced that this person was making her first steps onto the world online stage and having a much higher regard for her opinions than should otherwise awarded to her. Be careful what you say about people and businesses. Much better to keep quiet and have others suspect you are stupid rather than open your mouth and have it confirmed.

Chapter Thirty-nine

'OTAs – online travel agents'

There are a number of websites offering last minute rates and deals which present a level playing field for both guests and accommodation properties. In any case the same deals would, or should, be available on the accommodation operator's website without any additional booking charges and fees. In some cases, the same prices can still be available through normal travel agents who can do the searching for you. It is up to the individual of course to choose their preferred method of booking. My recommendation in all cases, regardless of how you do your research, would be to contact the establishment directly and talk to the owner, manager or reception.

By all means use the online listings to research the available accommodation, but when it comes to booking call the property to make the booking. Don't believe all the information you are presented with especially 'cross through' prices. The best deals will always be directly with the properties and if they (the property) are stupid enough not to match or better the advertised prices they deserve to either lose the booking or pay unnecessary commissions.

On the other side of the equation are bookings through travel agents and tour companies. Accommodation properties pay commissions to these organisations who in effect act as a selling agent because they speak with the clients and advise them based on information available or experience which would be the best property to suit their needs. There are some accommodation properties that reject paying commissions to these organisations however if it is business that you would normally not get then 80% of something is better than 100% of nothing.

In most cases travel agents and wholesalers bring in business that a property would otherwise not have access to. The internet is different in that smart accommodation properties have their own website and booking engine that enables them to be in the same space as the OTAs. In recent years another challenge are the paid ads to Google in particular which now fill up the first page, and sometimes more, ahead of the organic rankings of individual properties. Using Google listing ads to prioritise the first page rankings in Google would be outside the financial capabilities of individual small accommodation properties. In this regard the only way to beat this is to educate the public that OTAs are not the way to go even if they make it easy to plan itineraries on driving and touring holidays. Trivago in recent years has started to include the actual accommodation website and even indicates a lower price on some of their TV ads. Even so don't be sucked in by cross throughs and cheap 'lead in' prices. Before you make your booking check with the accommodation property first. If they are 'smart' they will either give you the best price, offer a free upgrade or offer inclusions such as breakfast or other free or discounted offers.

Tourism accommodation businesses don't have much choice. They need to be in the same space as potential clients and guests. Traditionally commissions were 10% from way back. Then the OTAs got greedy once they started getting large volumes of business. Bit by bit they will increase commissions while ever they are commanding volume market share. The small accommodation owner must ensure they get at least 50% of their business direct and commission free. Small scales of economy are very vulnerable to nett returns and with small business experiencing greater compliance and operating costs the margins they are working with are sensitive to say the least. The internet brought markets within reach that were previously costly to penetrate but they also brought with it the OTAs who seduce the customer to book through them instead of directly with the product. The OTAs make it easy and take some of the hard work out of sourcing a wide choice of available rooms and services. As a customer, use that resource and then book direct, interact with your host and get the satisfaction of knowing that both you and your host have made a mutually satisfactory arrangement.

One other very important reason to book directly with the supplier is that all of your purchase price goes into the local economy. You personally may not care too much about that, but it is vitally important to tourism destinations to retain as much revenue as possible so that the community gets maximum benefit out of your visit. Smiles all round.

Chapter Forty

'make the internet work for you'

The online environment is crucial to all tourism businesses. It is a complex component and I will only point out a few essentials in terms of advice. A tourism business will need a good website. If you are purchasing an existing tourism business, look very closely at the website and find out how long ago it was built. Today websites need to be optimised for use with mobile devices and this usually requires a re-build. Ensure this cost is in your budget. A good website with full function will cost $2000-$3000 and for that price it can be enabled for mobile use. A B&B would not need its own smartphone App but if the local or regional tourism association has a website or App then make sure you are part of it and become a member of their organisation. You will see down the track how worthwhile that will be.

Your business website should have its own booking button that allows live bookings to be made 24/7. There are several companies providing booking buttons for websites, and a few are outstandingly good. Make sure you use a fixed cost system and not a 'commission based' system for the booking button on your own website. You should also employ the use of a Channel Manager and I recommend you use the same company that provides your booking button. You will need to list with at least the top five online booking websites that will also be linked into your channel manager. There will be a variety of commissions involved but none should be over 15% and ensure that most of them are 10%. Any sites requiring more than 12% I would seriously consider not using.

Now having said all that if all you want to do is take life easy and have a few rooms that fill up every now and then; if money is of no concern and it will not worry you if you don't see any house guests for weeks on end then you don't need to do anything I have mentioned. However, lifestyle businesses still need to be run as a business otherwise the lifestyle can become expensive.

The essence of the hospitality and tourism industry is just that, hospitality. True hospitality comes from respect and whether you are a host or a guest if we all abide by that rule then we will all enjoy what we do whether we are at work or on holiday.

Rating systems

When we first opened, the automobile associations in Australia administered the star rating system for accommodation. Around 2000 the system was taken over in Australia by Star Ratings Australia. During the time we opened, and for several years after, RACT looked after it in Tasmania.   Each year an inspector would visit at our property and check we were meeting the requirements for the rating scheme. In addition, as we had a licensed establishment, the licencing commission would also inspect us. They would also check that our standards were being maintained. We started off with a '4.5 star' rating, and we upgraded to 5-star within a year when we installed independent temperature controls in each bedroom and bathroom. At that stage we were using a LPG/gas powered heating system which also had a fresh air setting. On the west coast of Tasmania temperatures rarely got high enough to warrant air conditioning although we did install it a few years later.

After Star Ratings Australia took over around 2000, there was the inevitable annual inspection and we quite expected to be taken down to 4.5 stars as the scheme was now Australia wide with new standards based on a national template. The new scheme basically put every property on the same scale which suited larger hotels and motels but put heritage guesthouses and B&Bs at a distinct disadvantage.

Our first inspection by the newly appointed inspector happened one fine day and she selected one of our rooms at random which was fine with us. The room in question was the Mary Alice room, resplendent with original antiques, a federation en-suite with a claw foot bath etc, etc. The room was an odd shape and the bed was an antique four poster c1860. It was smaller than a queen size bed, but I feel a little larger than a double. I would often say to guests when I showed them the room that the bed was 140 years old, but the mattress wasn't.

When we restored the house, we wanted the building to remain authentic. Unlike other restored properties that replaced architraves, windows and other features with new timbers we wanted to retain the essence of a heritage property. Thus, there were painted timber elements around the house that had the character of old features as old houses do. This was apparently not to the liking of our inspector who inspected the visible marks, nicks and scratches under the paintwork on the skirting boards and around the window architraves and other areas. We had utilised as much of the original timber work as we could even when we relocated doorways and established new ones using the original timbers and frames.

We got severely knocked down in points for any visible nicks and dings in the timbers. The antique bed received negative points due to its age and size as did the floor space within the room. The most ridiculous statement came when she examined the French dressing table with a bevelled oval mirror and beautiful inlaid parquetry. "You don't have a light above the mirror, that will cost you points, and the mirror is not large enough either. Also, you don't have any benches against the wall." I said, "Hang on a minute, French dressers didn't come with lights and I am not going to put another mirror on the wall as the wardrobe has a full-length mirror anyway, and what's this about a bench?"

She explained to me that bedrooms needed a bench with a mirror and light on the wall. I argued and said that is what a motel has not a heritage guesthouse. I then said, " Now tell me, if I took out the French dresser, which we paid nearly $3000 for, put an adhesive battery fluoro on the wall, got a laminated panel from the hardware store and an adhesive wall mirror from K Mart then we would get more points?"

She said yes you would.

I said, "Fuck off, we are no longer part of your star rating scheme, we will be self-rated from now on."

She scurried off with her tail between her legs saying that she could rate us at 4.5 stars if we agree to make the necessary changed within 12 months, otherwise we would be rated at 3.5 stars. I said, "you are not listening to me we no longer use your scheme."

The absence of a star rating made absolutely no difference. I did hear that sometime later the rating scheme was adapted to accommodate heritage style guesthouse and B&B

accommodation but by that stage many of us had dropped out of the star ratings system. In fact, our business increased quite exponentially whilst being self-rated and of course by that stage customers were more interested in guest reviews. In Tasmania it was more important to be accredited with the Tourism Industry Council which we were anyway. Although they were a pain in the backside, as each year they would bring in new criteria which in turn would increase our operating costs and give us more jobs to do just to keep them happy. In fact, if they just left us alone to do what we did best, that is, look after our guests, life would have been a lot better. There is too much regulation in life and business today. As Kerry Packer once said during a commission inquiry, "do you realise that every time you introduce a new law or regulation, you take away someone's liberty."

To B&B guests and owners ....*keep smiling and be nice to each other.*

About the Author

Mike Fry started his working life with the Royal Australian Navy in the radar division leaving in 1975 as a petty officer air control instructor. He entered the family supermarket business in Rockhampton, Queensland followed by two years with Uncle Bens as the central Queensland representative. In 1979 he joined the Airport Fire and Rescue service at the Rockhampton Airport until taking up a position with Bush Pilots Airways as their sales and port manager in 1981. Mike was responsible for the new Keppel Island transit service from Rockhampton Airport. This was during the highly successful 'Get Wrecked on Keppel Island' campaign. Mike was then posted to Brisbane as the Sales Manager for South East Queensland with Air Queensland (formerly BPA). In 1983 he purchased a 50% share in the Brisbane Paddlewheeler as an owner skipper until 1995 when he and partner Carolyn purchased Ormiston House in Strahan Tasmania. They restored and established a high-profile guesthouse and restaurant while at the same time being very active in regional tourism promotion. Mike was Chair of the regional tourism group from 1996-2003. The Chair of the local Strahan group from 2006-2009, and co-ordinator of Discover Strahan for a further five years. During his time at Strahan Mike was also a board member of ITOT. In addition to operating the guesthouse Mike also operated four-wheel drive tours and as a fishing guide for trout fishermen. Mike was known as an outspoken advocate for small tourism businesses in the region and worked extensively to build the brand and visitation to the west coast of Tasmania. The Ormiston House Book was written during the first five years at Ormiston House and is now in its 3rd edition. Mike and Carolyn sold

Ormiston House in 2012 and moved to Hobart in 2016 where they both continue to be connected to the tourism industry and where Mike concentrates on his writing and working with Huon pine in his home workshop.

www.ingramcontent.com/pod-product-compliance
Lightning Source LLC
Chambersburg PA
CBHW071637200326
41519CB00012BA/2333